Growing Ferns

An attractive corner fernery, *Cyathea cooperi* providing height and forming the main feature. It is surrounded by a range of smaller ferns providing contrasts in colour and texture

Growing Ferns

John Mason

Kangaroo Press

Acknowledgments

My sincere thanks to all who have assisted with the preparation of this book.

The mammoth and often frustrating task of making sense of the classification of ferns was undertaken with a great deal of help from Iain Harrison and Rosemary Lawrence, tutors with the Australian Horticultural Correspondence School. Their input into this book has been invaluable.

My gratitude to Annemarie Thomson and Iain Harrison for correcting my all too frequent errors in grammar and spelling.

Stephen Mason, my 13 year old son, continued to amaze us all with several of the drawings included in this book.

Photographs by my ever patient wife, Leonie, and myself. (The good ones are hers.)

And last, but not least, my thanks to you for taking the time to read this work. I trust it will be both rewarding and enjoyable.

John Mason

Reprinted in 1992
First published in 1990 by Kangaroo Press Pty Ltd
3 Whitehall Road (P.O. Box 75) Kenthurst 2156
Typeset by G.T. Setters Pty Limited
Printed in Hong Kong by Colorcraft Ltd

ISBN 0 86417 281 8

Contents

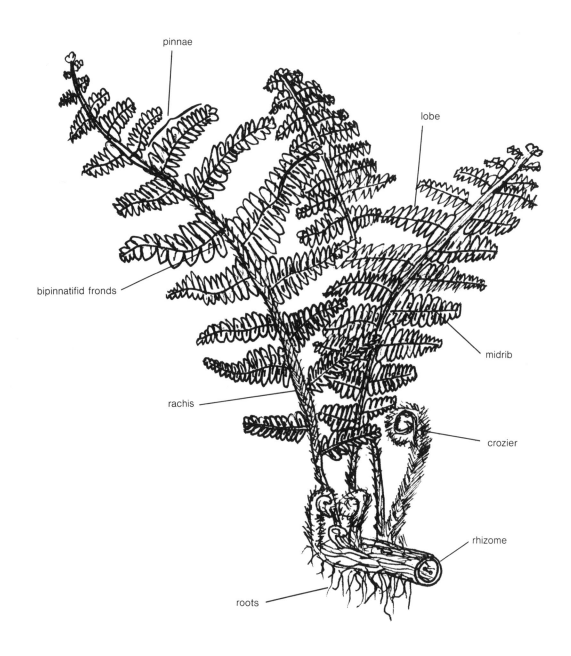

pinnae

lobe

bipinnatifid fronds

midrib

rachis

crozier

rhizome

roots

Parts of a typical fern

1 Discovering Ferns

There is a very special quality about ferns which conjures up images of coolness, calmness, peacefulness. They are graceful and lush, and have the potential to make a major contribution towards a relaxed and inviting feeling in any garden.

Ferns are popular as both garden and indoor plants. If you choose carefully the varieties you wish to grow, there is no reason why ferns cannot become some of your most successful and attractive plants.

Ferns don't have flowers like most other garden plants, and in many ways they are more like mosses than flowering plants. This lack of colourful flowers is more than made up for by the enormous variety to be found in plant size, foliage texture and colour.

Ferns as indoor plants

Many indoor plants suffer through a lack of light. Ferns are often the solution in this situation. Most (but not all) tolerate very poorly lit situations. They are generally ideal as indoor plants, both creating the aesthetic effect required and being able to deal with the indoor environment for a reasonable period of time without deteriorating. Remember though— neither ferns nor any other plants occur naturally inside buildings! Any indoor plant will sooner or later need a spell outside to rejuvenate itself.

Ferns as a solution for problem areas

Heavily shaded places and wet soggy sites in the garden are often problem areas which seem to defy solution. Everything you plant there seems to die. In both cases, ferns are often an excellent solution, most species being tolerant to both excessive moisture and shade. Just check on the varieties you want to use first though, as there are some which do not like these conditions.

There are varieties of fern to be found in all corners of the world, from the Arctic to the tropics, and on every continent except Antarctica. Even though we think of ferns as growing in wet places, this is not always so. Some species in fact thrive in dry climates. There are ferns which grow in coastal areas, exposed to severe winds and salt spray. There are varieties which are drought resistant, and others which tolerate extremes of heat or cold.

Generally those varieties which occur in harsher environments have developed special mechanisms for dealing with extreme conditions. Some are deciduous plants which die back to the roots when the weather becomes severe, then regrow when the season turns more favourable. Other ferns have small, thick, hard fronds to help them resist cold or wind. Drought resistant ferns frequently have a covering of scales or hairs which reduce the rate of water loss from the fronds. Many ferns survive dry conditions by growing their roots among and under rocks or logs where the soil remains cool and moist even on the hottest days.

Ferns are in fact one of the oldest groups of plants in existence. Fossil records show ferns existed over 400 million years ago. It is estimated that today there are around 11 500 species spread over 240 genera, making the ferns one of the largest groups of plants in the world.

Getting to know your ferns

The classification and identification of ferns is full of contradictions. Many of the experts around the world have conflicting viewpoints on what different ferns should be called. The information on ferns in this book, as in any other, will have some experts who agree with it and others who do not.

Unlike many other fern books, this book does not set out to give you a tool for identifying ferns. It aims to give you a broad understanding of each of the groups (or genera) which ferns belong to, and in this way to provide a very practical, easy-to-refer-to guide on how to grow most of the ferns you are likely to come across.

Ferns can be grouped under five broad headings—terrestrial filmy ferns, terrestrial tree ferns, rock ferns, epiphytic ferns and water ferns.

Terrestrial filmy ferns

This group have fronds one cell thick. They can occur only in wet or misty areas. This group includes Apteropteris, Cephalomanes, Crepidomanes, Gonocormus, Hymenophyllum, Macroglena, Microgonium, Microtrichomanes, Pleuromanes, Polyphlebium, Reediella, Selenodesmium, Sphaerocionium and Trichomanes.

- In the Apteropteris group the fern fronds have a dense covering of stellate hairs.
- The Cephalomanes group can be identified by a tufted rhizome and pinnate fronds with a harsh texture.
- The Crepidomanes group have narrow segments with false veins. Their rhizome is filiform.
- The Gonocormus group have very narrow segments with venation.
- With Hymenophyllum, the lips of the indusium are proportionately longer than the base.

Water garden incorporating ferns and other plants

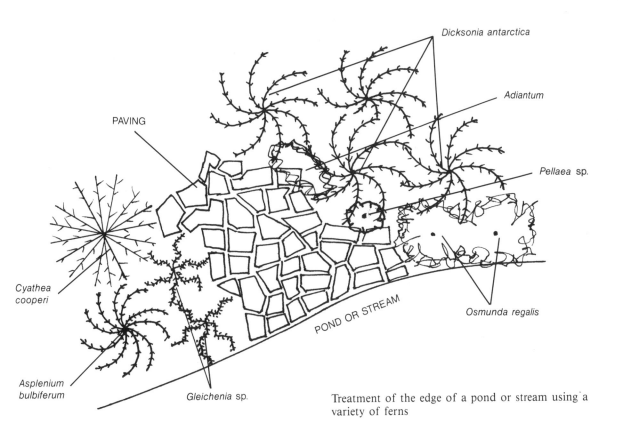

Dicksonia antarctica

Adiantum

PAVING

Pellaea sp.

Cyathea
cooperi

POND OR STREAM

Osmunda regalis

Asplenium
bulbiferum

Gleichenia sp.

Treatment of the edge of a pond or stream using a variety of ferns

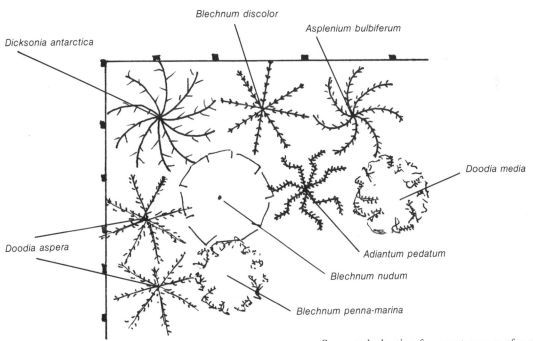

Blechnum discolor

Asplenium bulbiferum

Dicksonia antarctica

Doodia media

Doodia aspera

Adiantum pedatum

Blechnum nudum

Blechnum penna-marina

Suggested planting for a wet corner of a garden in semi-shade using ferns (NB: These are all hardy in temperate to cold climates)

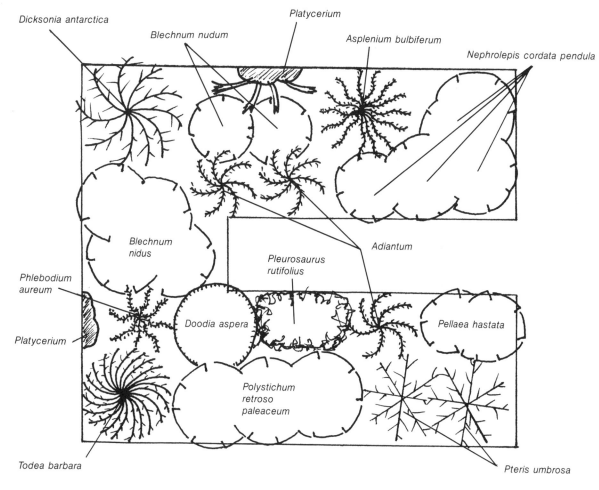

Dicksonia antarctica

Blechnum nudum

Platycerium

Asplenium bulbiferum

Nephrolepis cordata pendula

Blechnum
nidus

Pleurosaurus
rutifolius

Adiantum

Phlebodium
aureum

Platycerium

Doodia aspera

Pellaea hastata

Polystichum
retroso
paleaceum

Todea barbara

Pteris umbrosa

Suggested planting for a 5 m × 6 m shaded fernery

Terrestrial tree ferns

The most obvious feature of these ferns is their woody upright trunk or caudex. At least part of the trunk is made up of masses of aerial roots which if covered by soil tend to grow out to produce a root system. The trunk is topped by a crown of long divided fronds. There are two main groups, Cyathea and Dicksonia, although Cyathea is frequently broken up into several other genera.

In Cyathea the caudex is erect and stout or slender, and the young developing fronds are covered with scales on all surfaces.

The Dicksonia group are regarded as more primitive, since no scales are produced, but the young fronds are covered with stiff fine hairs. The stipes are smooth and lack the rough protuberances usually found on Cyatheas.

Rock ferns

This group contains the genera Bommeria, Cheilanthes, Goniophlebium and Pleurosorus. Members of the Bommeria have distinct hairy fronds.

Members of the Cheilanthes group are found almost world-wide throughout the tropics and subtropics. Members of this group are able to withstand dry conditions, having small finely divided fronds and protective coverings of hairs and scales. Some are able to shrivel but recover when moisture becomes available. The rock ferns in the genus Goniophlebium have long weeping fronds; rock ferns in genus Pleurosorus are small, have short rhizomes and are clad in clathrate scales.

Epiphytic ferns

Epiphytic ferns grow in the air, attached to another plant, but are not parasitic on that plant. Some epiphytes will also grow in dead or decomposing organic material on the ground.

Though there are exceptions, epiphytic ferns tend to be spreading and have long drooping fronds. Genera in this group include the Aglaomorpha, Antrophyum, Campyloneurum, Cephalomanes, Davallodes, Gonophlebium, Humata, Lecanopteris, Macroglena, Microsorum, Microtrichomanes, Niphidium, Platycerium, Pleuromanes, Polypodium, Polyphlebium, Reediella, Selleguea and Trichomanes.

Members of the group Aglaomorpha have thick scaly rhizomes, members of the Antrophyum have tufted rhizomes, Campyloneurum may be identified by entire strap-like fronds, Cephalomanes members have harsh-textured fronds and tufted rhizomes, Davallodes are known as haresfoot ferns because they have scaly rhizomes, Goniophlebium have creeping rhizomes, Humata members have leathery fronds, Lecanopteris may be recognised by hollow fleshy rhizomes, Macroglena members can be identified by very fine bristle-like ultimate segments, Microsorum members have simple strap-like fronds.

Microtrichomanes have either simple or forked brownish fronds. Niphidium members can be identified as medium sized ferns with simple fronds; members of the Platycerium group have drooping, easily spreading fronds.

The Pleuromanes may be identified by broad bipinnate fronds, which may be grey, glaucous or white. These fronds are covered with a waxy powder. The Polyphlebium members have broad segments with freely branching veins. The members of the Polypodium group have short creeping rhizomes, members of the Reediella are small with upright fronds with one or two rows of marginal cells thickened to form a border. Members of Selleguea have creeping rhizomes, members of the Trichomanes have thick rhizomes and erect fronds on long stipes bearing no veins.

Water ferns

There are two distinct groups of water ferns, the Salviniales (e.g. *Azolla*) and the Marsileales (e.g. *Pilularia* and *Marsilea*).

The fronds of *Pilularia* are very small and similar in appearance to a grass; *Marsilea* has fronds similar to a four leaf clover. The Salviniales have tiny overlapping leaves borne alternately on branching stems.

All water ferns grow in shallow water and where they are periodically flooded may grow as annuals.

2 How to Grow Ferns

To get the most out of your ferns you must provide the best possible conditions for their growth. As there are thousands of different types of ferns, from many different types of environments, be wary of generalising too much about what conditions are best for your ferns. While most ferns may very well prefer wet shaded conditions, there are many exceptions, with some ferns being adapted to quite arid conditions, open sunny positions and even exposure to salty ocean spray. To grow such species in your garden or home generally requires that you provide similar conditions to those that they normally experience in their natural habitats. It is important to remember that these plants have adapted or evolved to grow in specific conditions over thousands or even millions of years and are often very precise in the conditions they require, although some may prove quite adaptable.

To fully understand the conditions for growth that a fern requires, you should first carefully read the information label generally supplied when you purchase a fern. If a label is not supplied you may need to obtain your information directly from the person who supplied the plant. Other useful sources are your local fern society or club and the extensive plant directory provided in this book.

While remembering the previous warning about overgeneralising on growing conditions for ferns, there are a number of general rules that can be applied to the majority of ferns commonly cultivated.

Situation

Most ferns do best in a situation where they are protected from strong winds, extremes of temperature and excessive dryness.

Ferns growing in containers are usually best placed on a shaded verandah or patio or underneath some large trees where they will only receive filtered sunlight.

Ferns growing in the ground are normally best with moist soil in semi-shade to full shade. If there is any likelihood of the ground drying out, a heavy organic mulch is recommended.

Greenhouses may be needed to provide shade protection for growing ferns, particularly in warmer climates. Shadehouses need to have shade cloth (or something else) on the sides as well as on the roof to break strong winds.

Adequate ventilation is generally important to minimise fungal infections. This can be achieved by not placing plants too close together, and by ensuring that there is some air movement, particularly through greenhouses. Too much air movement, however, can also be a problem.

Soils and potting mixes

Ferns are only as good as the soil they are growing in. If you want quality plants you must use quality soils or potting mixes. Ferns are generally adaptable as far as soil type goes, but a soil that is well drained, well aerated, has a reasonable pH, has high organic matter and good moisture holding capacity is preferred by most. For container growing of ferns, or even in specially prepared beds, potting mixes can provide an excellent substitute for the fern's natural soil type.

There are basically two types of potting mixes—those which contain soil and those which don't.

The essential consideration for a potting mix is that it should drain freely. To test this, fill a pot with your soil mix and dip it into a bucket of water. If the water moves away quickly, then it is acceptable—if it does not, then either the soil requires more sand (or similar drainage material) in it, or possibly the pot just doesn't have sufficient drainage holes in it.

Soilless potting mixes have the advantage of being cleaner than those which contain soil, i.e. soil can contain weed seeds, insects, fungi and other harmful pathogens. A soilless mix has much less chance of having these problems. Soilless mixes are more likely not to contain the necessary nutrients found in soil mixes—this means that well balanced fertilisers usually need to be added to them.

Components of a typical soilless mix might include fine shredded (and weathered) pine bark, coarse washed sand, scoria, vermiculite, perlite, rice hulls, old sawdust.

Soil mixes usually contain a mixture of different types of soils, and perhaps some soilless components.

Components

The characteristic of a particular potting mix is a blend of the various components which make up that mix. The components which are used in higher proportions have the greatest impact on the mix. You can modify the characteristics of your mixes to suit individual plant variety requirements by adding more of a component which has the desired qualities, e.g. if you want a mix to hold more water, add more peat moss because that holds water well; if you want it to drain better, add more sand because that improves drainage.

1. Peat moss

Peat moss, though expensive, is one of the best components for fern potting mixes. The pH of peat is generally around 4.5 (i.e. very acidic), which is too low for many ferns. This level may be raised by the addition of other components, though lime may also need to be added if growing varieties which require alkaline conditions. Peat has both excellent drainage and water holding characteristics, but problems can arise if it becomes too dry, as dry peat moss is difficult to rewet.

2. Sphagnum moss

Sphagnum moss is most commonly used in lining hanging baskets and behind epiphytes mounted onto slabs. It has excellent moisture holding characteristics and has the ability to inhibit the development of fungal diseases. Its main disadvantage is its high cost.

3. Perlite

This lightweight material derived from a volcanic rock looks like small hard spongy white balls. It holds water very well and drains well. It is sterile and has a pH of around 7 to 7.5. Perlite can be purchased from large nurseries and hydroponic suppliers.

4. Vermiculite

This is another mineral material (derived from mica), which appears as spongy flakes or granules. It has the ability to absorb and hold large quantities of water, making it a useful additive to mixes, but can be a problem if used in too high a proportion. Never use more than 30% vermiculite in a mix.

5. Coarse sand

This is the same as propagating or aquarium sand, sold in some nurseries, in aquarium shops and in some soil supply yards. It is sometimes added to mixes which are predominantly peat, perlite or vermiculite to improve drainage. It can be useful in providing weight to a light mix—where plant foliage is large and soil is light, pots will fall over very easily.

6. Pine bark

Pine bark is an inexpensive substitute for peat moss. It has many of the same properties as peat, provided it is graded properly and *well composted* before use. If shortcuts are taken during composting, toxic chemicals remaining in the bark in extreme cases will kill many ferns. The bark should be shredded and graded to a uniform particle size. If there is too

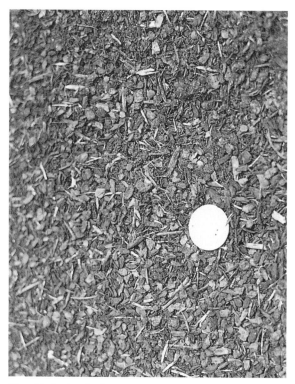

Shredded pine bark

bacteria to work. To speed up the rate of composting, you need the following conditions:

(a) The level of moisture in the heap should always remain the same as a squeezed sponge (never wetter or drier—around 40% to 60% moisture).

(b) The temperature in the heap should be around 50 to 55°C. This is best achieved by keeping the heap between 1 and 2 metres in length, width and height. The bacteria will generate that level of temperature in that sized heap.

(c) The level of oxygen in the heap should be high. To achieve this the heap must be turned every few weeks.

(d) The organic material used must be balanced. Too high a level of nitrogen (found in manures, for example) or too low a level of nitrogen (as in sawdust or paper), will slow the rate of composting considerably.

9. Other additives

A range of other things can be used in fern potting mixes, e.g. rice hulls, pumice, composted sawdust, sandy loam.

much variation in particle size, there will be considerable variation throughout the potting mix and water holding characteristics may vary greatly from one side to the other of the same pot.

7. Leaf mould

Leaf litter or partially decomposed leaves are excellent for mulching ferns, digging into soil or even adding to potting mixes. Leaves from most deciduous trees (particularly oaks) are very good. Eucalypt and conifer leaves contain toxic chemicals which must be leached away during a period of composting before they are used.

8. Compost

Compost is made by heaping organic material (sometimes including soil) into piles and decomposing the material before using it. When compost decomposes, the pH will initially drop to a low level, and then return close to where it started from as the process nears completion. The composting process can take anything from 2 to 12 months or more, according to whether or not the conditions are appropriate for the decomposing

Potting mixes suitable for growing ferns.

1. A general soilless mix:
>   6 parts peat moss
>   2 parts vermiculite
>   1 part coarse sand

2. A pine bark/soil mix:
>   7 parts 3 mm hammermilled composted pine bark
>   2 parts sterilised sandy loam
>   1 part peat moss

3. A compost based mix:
>   2 parts compost or leaf mould
>   1 part coarse sand
>   1 part perlite

4. A potting mix for epiphytic ferns:
>   1 part chunky pine bark (approx. 10–20 mm)
>   1 part coarse sand
>   2 parts peat moss

5. An alternative potting mix for epiphytic ferns:

    1 part tree fern fibre
    1 part charcoal
    1 part peanut shells or rice hulls
    1 part 6 mm composted pine bark or peat
    moss

Preparing for planting

Before planting ferns out into the ground, the soil must be properly prepared. Remember, the soil should be high in organic matter and reasonably well drained. Most soils will benefit from large quantities of manure and compost being dug in before planting. A reasonable approach would be as follows:

1. Dig over (or rotary hoe the soil first).
2. Spread compost, wood shavings or fine shredded pine bark to a depth of 200 mm and dig this in to a depth of 400 mm.
3. Spread well rotted poultry or cow manure over the area to a depth of 50 mm and dig in to a depth of 200 mm.
4. Water well and leave for at least 2 weeks.
5. Spray any weeds which begin to germinate with Zero or Roundup weedicide, and leave for another week.
6. Plant the ferns and cover with a surface mulch 100 mm thick.

Maintenance

Feeding

Most ferns do need to be fed from time to time, though as a general rule they are more susceptible to fertiliser burn than many other types of plants. If you stick to the following recommendations you are unlikely to have any major problems:

- Use fertilisers twice as often as recommended, but at *half* the recommended rate.
- Never get the fertiliser on the foliage—always apply it to the soil under the fronds.
- Don't dig the fertiliser in (ferns are happiest not having their roots disturbed).

- Water the fertiliser in well as soon as it is applied, to prevent concentrated lumps making direct contact with any exposed surface roots.
- Organic liquid fertilisers such as Maxicrop plant food, Seasol, Nitrosol or Garden Party are ideal for ferns, being less likely to burn than inorganic fertilisers.
- Slow release fertilisers such as Dynamic Lifter or Osmocote are also excellent for ferns.
- Check what has been written about the variety of fern you are dealing with before you feed it. Some varieties should *never* be fertilised. There are other varieties which require heavier feeding than the average fern. Watch the fronds of the heavy feeders—if they go pale in colour, or if the growth rate slows, you can increase the feeding by up to 30%.

What nutrients does a fern need?

All plants need a range of different nutrients not just to grow, but also to remain healthy.

The following nutrients are needed in large amounts: nitrogen, phosphorus, potassium (also called potash), calcium and magnesium. These are called *major nutrients*.

A large number of other nutrients are needed in much smaller quantities, including iron, sulphur, manganese, boron, zinc, copper, molybdenum, chlorine, cobalt and sodium. These are called *minor nutrients*.

Most soils will contain all that a plant needs of calcium, magnesium and the minor nutrients. Fertilisers therefore are usually designed to supply mainly nitrogen, potassium and phosphorus, the nutrients most commonly needed.

Complications!

The fact that a nutrient exists in a soil does not necessarily mean that the plant can absorb and use it. If the pH (level of acidity) is wrong, the plant can have a lot of difficulty absorbing some of the required nutrients even if they are there in abundant supply. For this reason the soil pH is an extremely critical factor in growing some types of fern. You can measure the pH with a pH test kit available from most good nurseries. (The chemical test kit is more accurate than the inexpensive pH test meters.) These kits usually have excellent instructions not only on how to use them, but also on how to adjust the soil pH after you have tested it.

Is your fern underfed?

If a fern is underfed, the foliage will often become lighter in colour. If the older fronds become very pale, the fern probably has a nitrogen deficiency, in which case a good feed may help. Other symptoms of nutrient deficiency includes a loss of vigour in the growth and increased susceptibility to disease.

Is your fern suffering fertiliser burn?

In extreme cases the youngest, most tender foliage will burn at the tips if too much fertiliser has been applied. If you dig up a few young roots and examine the growing tips, fertiliser burn will often show as discoloration or dying back on the growing root tips. (Overwatering can result in similar symptoms.) If the plant is in a pot, simply remove it from the pot to make a quick examination of the roots.

The only way to treat a plant which has been given too much fertiliser is to leach the fertiliser away. For a container plant extra waterings may help. For a plant in the ground, often only time will help it gradually recover.

Remember it is easier to put fertiliser on than to take it off.

Pruning

Ferns are pruned for the following reasons:

1. *To remove dead or diseased fronds.* These look unsightly and detract from the overall appearance of the plant. More importantly, diseased fronds encourage disease to spread to healthy parts of that plant, or other plants nearby. Dead or diseased fronds should be removed or burnt.

2. *To control the size of the plant.* Large ferns can spread and impose on other parts of the garden. In such cases they are pruned back simply to control their size.

3. *To promote new growth.* If older, perhaps marked or unsightly fronds are removed, a flush of new lush growth will be stimulated. You may choose to take such action to bring your plants to looking their best for a particular occasion.

Whenever you prune, be sure to use sharp tools, and always cut the leaf stalk right back to the base. A clean cut will heal, a rough cut is likely to become diseased.

Woodshavings mulch is inexpensive and ideal for keeping the soil both moist and cool

Mulching

For the vast majority of ferns, there are four major advantages to mulching:

1. It keeps the roots cool in warm weather.
2. It keeps the soil moist during the drier part of the year.
3. It controls weed growth which might compete with the ferns.
4. It replenishes nutrients in the soil.

There are many different types of mulches available, e.g. horticultural fabrics, gravels, stone, organic mulches, but only the organic mulches will provide all four benefits listed above.

The best organic mulches for ferns are peat moss, sphagnum moss, compost, leaf litter or something similar. Unfortunately these are also the most expensive or more difficult to obtain materials. Less expensive alternatives are shredded pine bark, red gum chips or wood shavings. These materials should not be used too fresh, needing to be weathered for at least three months in wet conditions to eliminate toxins.

Ferns will respond to mulching at least once annually, in early spring. The mulch should be applied to between 10 and 20 cm thickness.

Thinning and replanting

Some clump forming ferns, e.g. *Nephrolepis cordata*, can over a period form such a dense clump that they become choked with roots and foliage in the centre. The fern can become depleted of nutrients and water absorption into the root zone can be restricted. In such a case it is advisable to dig up the clump, build up the soil by digging in compost or manure, for example, and replant smaller divisions throughout the area.

Some ferns, e.g. Athyrium, can over a period of time develop a crown which raises the fern up out of the ground. When this happens, the fern must either be dug up and replanted deeper into the soil, or mulched heavily to cover up the exposed crown. New roots will emerge from the covered section.

Watering

All plants need water to grow and to survive. The amount of water needed, however, varies from plant to plant. The two main things which affect how much water a plant needs are its variety and its environment.

Some varieties of plants have the ability to retain water within their tissues for later use. Other plants are unable to do this.

If the environment in which the plant is growing makes plenty of water available around it, then it is unlikely to suffer from a lack of water. Shaded, cool situations tend to remain more moist than exposed, windy, sunny situations.

A plant can suffer from a lack of water. A plant can also suffer from an excessive amount of water. It is important to strike the delicate balance between too little and too much. Overwatering can be just as bad as underwatering.

Symptoms of water deficiency

The first symptom is usually a slowing in the rate of growth. This is usually in a mild case, only a slight deficiency. As the water deficiency becomes greater, stems become slender, fronds become smaller, and wilting occurs. In extreme water deficiency the tips of the plant can die back, and the whole plant may eventually die.

Symptoms of water excess

Seedlings can become leggy if they are planted close together, and/or if there is too much moisture about. Plant tissue cells can become enlarged; in extreme cases they can burst. Internodes become elongated, i.e. the spaces between two leaves on a stem become elongated, stretched out. In extreme situations fronds can blacken, plants can die back or die off completely.

Maintaining appropriate water levels

To maintain appropriate water levels, first consider the soil where a plant is growing. If the plant is getting too wet, perhaps the soil should drain more freely. If the plant is getting too dry, perhaps the soil's moisture retaining qualities need enhancing.

Consider the frequency of watering. Maybe you need to water more often or less often.

Consider water penetration. Does the water you apply absorb into the soil or does it run off? Does the water land on the leaves of plants, being deflected away from the soil? Does the sun or wind evaporate the water before the plant gets to use it?

Is the plant in a shaded situation? Is it in a very hot place? How much natural rainfall has it been getting?

How to water

Watering lightly and often is undesirable in most situations. A light watering will never penetrate much below the surface of the soil. If only the very surface is wet, the soil dries out quickly through loss to the air above. When the deeper soil remains drier than the surface, plant roots tend to remain near the surface, making the plant less able to extract water from the deeper subsoil when the surface dries rapidly in hot weather.

The best way to wet the soil deeply is with a cyclic watering method. Water the soil until water begins to run off the surface—at this point the pore spaces near the surface are full of water. Any excess at this point will build up above the surface. After a while, excess water in the top layers soaks into the lower layers of the soil, leaving some free pore space again in the top soil. At this point the area can be watered again until runoff point is reached a second time. The whole process, if repeated several times, will continue to cause water penetration to a greater and greater depth in the soil.

Cyclic watering is appropriate in all but sandy soils.

Trickle irrigation

Trickle or drip irrigation involves delivering water to the plants through very fine tubes or drippers which water very slowly, that is, a slow drip or trickle is applied over a long period of time. Drip systems are easy to install and can be purchased in kit form from most hardware stores and large nurseries.

A properly designed trickle system will ensure minimum wastage of water and maximum penetration into the soil.

Trickle pipes and tubes, being made of low density plastics, are flexible and easy to hide among rocks and plants. Laterals can be buried and outlets placed in very obscure positions if desired. Not burying the laterals gives great flexibility to the system, as outlets can be moved at will.

Unlike sprinkler irrigation, the distribution of water by trickle irrigation is not interfered with by nearby shrubs and trees. Water can be delivered precisely to the base of each plant where it is needed.

3 In the Greenhouse

Many ferns, particularly the tropical varieties, can benefit greatly from being grown in a greenhouse. Obviously temperature control is the major benefit, but not so obvious is the high humidity created in a greenhouse, which is for some varieties of fern a critical factor in their success.

A greenhouse is only as good as its user. You can grow all sorts of plants in a greenhouse, and achieve all types of things which you might not be able to achieve otherwise, whether growing as a hobby or commercially. The greenhouse is only a tool though; a tool which enables you to keep your plants a little warmer and perhaps control a few other aspects of their growing conditions. You must know what conditions the plant needs and try to create those conditions within the greenhouse, adjusting the way you are managing it if conditions start to vary.

You need to decide what you will grow in the greenhouse, and be aware that different plants have different requirements. It may not be possible to grow a great variety of plants in the greenhouse and get the very best out of each one if each of those plants has different growth requirements.

Greenhouses are used to control the environment in which plants grow. The environment is extremely complex though, and there are many interactions between its different aspects. The amount of light allowed to get to the plants might affect the temperature. If you close the vents or doors of a glasshouse, you may stop the temperature from dropping, but at the same time you may be changing the balance of gases in the air. Every time you interfere to alter one thing, you end up altering a number of things.

Greenhouse management involves giving careful consideration to the full implications of every action you take.

Environmental factors influencing plant growth

1. Atmospheric temperature—the air.
2. Root zone temperature—the soil or hydroponic medium which the plant roots are growing in.
3. Water temperature—the water you irrigate the plants with.
4. Light conditions—shaded, full light, dark.
5. Atmospheric gas—plants give off oxygen but take in carbon dioxide. Animals do the reverse. Normally they balance each other, but when plants are locked in a closed room or house by themselves they become starved for carbon dioxide as the oxygen level in the enclosed space rises.
6. Air movement—mixes gases, evens out temperature.
7. Atmospheric moisture—humidity. N.B.: Very few ferns will grow in low humidity.
8. Root zone moisture—water levels in the soil or growing medium.

Tree ferns in shadehouse made from brush timbers at Footscray City Council, Victoria

A tunnel greenhouse, ideal for propagation or protected growing in temperate climates

Plant needs

Every variety of plant has its own specific needs and tolerances within the environment in which it grows. The horticulturist talks about 'optimum' conditions, 'tolerated conditions' and conditions which are 'not tolerated'. Let's talk about temperature conditions as an example.

Optimum conditions The conditions in which the plant grows best. Some plants have a wide optimum range. Some of the hardier temperate climate ferns will grow very well anywhere between 16 and 25°C. The most tender varieties of ferns, however, have a very limited optimum range, perhaps between 21 and 24°C.

Tolerated conditions Conditions under which the plant will survive, but not necessarily grow. Hardy fern varieties can tolerate temperatures below 0°C, and over 35°C. Some of the tender tropical ferns cannot tolerate temperatures below 16°C.

Not tolerated If conditions go outside the tolerated range, normally the plant would die.

Note These same principles apply equally to light, moisture and other environmental factors.

What can you grow?

Greenhouses are normally used to propagate new plants, as they provide the ideal conditions for spores to germinate or to initiate the growth of roots on cuttings; to grow tropical plants in cooler climates; to protect plants which are cold or frost sensitive over winter, or to grow plants more quickly than they might be grown outside.

There may be other uses, but these are the main ones.

Greenhouses and other growing structures

Greenhouses, hotbeds, coldframes, misting systems and so on are all types of equipment we use to aid propagation *or* to aid plant growth by providing some type of control over their environment.

Greenhouses

Any type of walk-in building which maintains an atmosphere suitable for good plant growth. Greenhouses fall into the following categories:
Glasshouses Glass walls (at least in part), very effective, long lasting, expensive.
Fibreglass houses Fibreglass sheet, cheaper, medium lifespan, poorly insulated.
Coreflute/solar sheet houses Medium cost, medium lifespan (15 years plus), more effective temperature control than PVC or fibreglass.
PVC film (polythene houses) Polythene film over a metal framework (usually a tunnel). Very cheap, lasts only a few years then requires cover replacement, poorer insulation than others.

Hotbeds

Heat is provided in the base of a bed (box arrangement) by means of electric heating cables, hot water or steam pipes, or hot air flues. The bed must have drainage outlets and be made from a material which will not rot (brick, concrete, treated timber, etc.). An ideal size is 1 m × 2 m. The hotbed is filled with 8 to 10 cm of coarse propagating sand or perlite.

Hotbed used for propagation. Hot water pipes embedded in concrete benches heat the roots of plants or germinating spore placed there

Hotbed and misting system, useful for propagation

Coldframes

A coldframe is almost identical to a hotbed except that it is not heated and it has a cover/top made from glass, plastic, fibreglass or some similar material. Coldframes can be set up inside or outside a greenhouse. A simple coldframe can be built for a very low cost and can be used effectively to strike cuttings or germinate spore (though it is not as effective as other structures).

Shadehouses

Used for protecting young plants, usually after removal from the propagating area or for providing the reduced light intensity needed to grow some species. Shadehouses allow for plants to be gradually eased out of their highly protected propagating environment to the harsher outside.

Mist systems

These involve a series of mist producing sprinklers which spray the plants at controlled intervals. They serve to prevent drying out and to keep the plants cool in the leaf zone.

Coldframe

A simple shadehouse—shadecloth supported by metal hoops

Temperature control

The temperature of a greenhouse can be controlled in several ways.

The *sun* will warm the greenhouse during the day. This effect varies according to the time of year, time of day and the weather conditions that day. The way the greenhouse is built and the materials used in construction will also influence its ability to catch heat from the sun, and hold that heat.

Heaters can be used to add to the heat in a house. The heater must have the ability to replace heat at the same rate at which it is being lost to the outside.

Vents and doors can be opened to let cool air into the greenhouse, or closed to stop warm air from escaping.

Shadecloth can be drawn over the house to stop the warm sun penetrating, or removed to allow the sun to heat the house. (Greenhouse paints—whitewash—can be applied in spring for the same

effect. The type of paint used is normally one which will last the summer, but wash off with weathering to allow penetration of warming light in winter.)

Coolers (blowers, etc.) can be used to lower temperature.

Watering or misting systems can be used to lower temperature.

Exhaust fans can be used to lower temperature.

Water storage under the floor or benches of a glasshouse can act as a buffer to temperature fluctuations.

Heat loss

An important consideration in temperature control is the heat lost through the walls and the roof of the house. Different types of materials (glass, plastic, etc.) have differing levels of ability to retain heat. Heat is normally measured in BTUs (British Thermal Units). The table on the next page provides some insight into the respective qualities of different materials.

Covering material	Heat loss (BTU/sq. ft/hr)
Glass (¼ inch)	1.13
Double layer glass	0.65
Fibreglass reinforced plastic	1.00
Acrylic sheet (3 mm thick)	1.00
Polythene film	1.15
Polythene film (double layer)	0.70
Polyester film	1.05

From *Greenhouse Operation* by Nelson, Prentice Hall.

Heaters

There are two main types of heating systems.

Centralised heating systems

Normally a boiler or boilers in one location generating steam or hot water which is piped to one or more greenhouse complexes. This is usually the most expensive type to install and may be more expensive to operate. There are side benefits though (e.g. the steam generated can be used to sterilise soils, pots, etc.). This type of system is only appropriate in large nurseries.

Localised heating systems

Often uses several individual heaters, normally blowing hot air into the greenhouse. Hot air is generally distributed through a plastic tube or sleeve, 30–60 cm in diameter, which is hung from the roof and has holes cut at calculated intervals for even distribution of warm air.

The main types of localised heaters are:

Unit heaters

Unit heaters consist of three parts.
1. Fuel is burnt in the *firebox* to provide heat at the bottom of the unit. The fuel is usually gas or oil.
2. Heat rises through a set of thin walled metal *tubes* or *pipes*, which heat up. There is an exhaust outlet for fumes above this.
3. Behind the heated tubes is a *fan* which blows cold air through the pipes out the other side into the house.

Convection heaters

These are cheap to purchase and are frequently used by hobbyists and small commercial growers. They differ from unit heaters in that they do not have a built-in heat exchanger.

Fuel of almost any type can be combusted in the firebox (wood, coal, gas, oil, etc.). Hot fumes then pass out of an exhaust pipe which can be placed between rows of plants, above the heater, or wherever you wish. The exhaust pipe should be sufficiently long (or outlets placed far enough away from plants), to ensure that dangerously hot air does not come in contact with the plants. A metal stovepipe or insulated ducting is ideal, however, polythene tubing can be used as well.

A potbelly stove or something similar could be used as a convection heater.

Electric heaters

In some parts of Australia, electricity is relatively cheap. If you happen to have a cheap supply, an electric heater may be worth considering. These generally consist of a heating element and a fan which blows air across the heating element and into the glasshouse. This type of heater can cost as little as 2 cents per hour to operate, but in some places as much as 15 cents or more.

Radiant heaters

Low energy infrared radiant heaters have become popular in the USA in recent years. Growers report significant savings on fuel costs.

Solar heaters

Several different types of solar heaters can be used or adapted for use in greenhouse heating. The basic components of a solar heater are a collector, a heat store and a heat exchanger.

Different types of *collector* are possible. They are usually panels heated by direct sunlight. The front is transparent to allow light in, the back is black and insulated to stop energy escaping. Light is converted to heat when it is absorbed by the dark surface.

Water and rocks are two of the most common *heat stores*. Water can be passed through the collector and returned to a storage tank of water. Air can pass through the collector and return to a storage tank of rocks.

The pipes or tubes of the *heat exchanger* can pass through the heat store, through the greenhouse and back to complete the cycle. A heat exchange fluid, or perhaps air, can flow through these pipes.

A backup heater may need to be used in conjunction with a solar system.

4 Problems

Ferns, like any other plant or animal, are susceptible to pest, disease and environmental problems which you are certain to encounter sooner or later. This is a fact that even the most proficient fern experts cannot escape. The best way to control such problems is to prevent them in the first place. The initial step in achieving this is to buy or obtain only healthy plants. Keeping your plants healthy by providing the correct growth conditions will allow your ferns to resist attack by pests and diseases and to withstand sudden changes in environmental conditions that might seriously damage or kill a weaker plant.

Prevention also includes maintaining good hygienic conditions. Equipment such as secateurs should be sterilised, after pruning or trimming each plant, in something like Dettol, methylated spirits or Biogram. Any pots, planters and propagating trays which are to be reused should have all traces of plants, potting mixes and soils removed, and then be washed in Pine-O-Clean, Dettol or Biogram, followed by flushing in clean water.

Any infected material should also be removed from garden beds or the propagating area and if possible destroyed. By reducing the likelihood of healthy plants coming in contact with infected material you greatly reduce the likelihood of problems occurring.

Another important control method is regular inspection of your plants. Problems caught early are usually easily overcome. In many cases small outbreaks of pests or diseases can be removed easily by hand before they have a chance to spread all over the plant or to other plants, or the problem may require the use of only a small amount of a chemical spray rather than a large amount, a situation most people would prefer.

While preventative techniques will reduce the chance of problems occurring it is still likely, however, that your ferns will suffer at some stage from one or other of many problems. In fact, hundreds of things can go wrong with your plants, but in most cases the problem is likely to be one of the common ones discussed below.

Aphids
Aphids are small insects which cluster in large numbers on the tender growth of plants, sucking juices through a sharp beak which they inject into the plant tissue. They can have serious effects, transmitting diseases from plant to plant, among other things. A spray with pyrethrum (a natural insecticide) will normally control aphids. In severe infestations you may need to use a stronger chemical such as malathion.

Scale insects
Scales are shield-like insects which attach themselves to plant tissue and feed on the plant below. Scale insects give off a sugary substance which attracts

snail

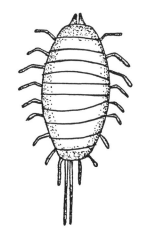

mealy bug

thrip

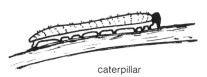

caterpillar

aphis

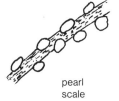

pearl
scale

cottony
cushion
scale

black
scale

Insect pests of ferns

ants (a telltale sign of their presence). This sugar or honey dew, as it is known, frequently provides food for the development of 'sooty mould', a black dust-like fungus which can make a plant quite unsightly. All three problems (ants, sooty mould and scale) are eliminated if you eliminate the scale.

The easiest way to control scale is with a suffocating spray of white oil. Covering these insects with a thin layer of the oil prevents them from breathing and hence they die. A related soft scale-like group of insects, known as mealybugs, which appear as small cotton-like tufts, can be treated in a similar way or by dipping a cloth in alcohol or methylated spirits and touching each individual insect.

White fly

White fly is a small flying insect which feeds on the underside of fronds. They can cause severe discoloration and reduce vigour. Systemic insecticides such as Rogor or Disyston are the only sure way to control white fly.

Thrip

Thrip are small black insects, barely visible without a magnifying glass. They can attack a range of ferns causing discoloration and loss of vigour. Rogor or malathion are the most effective treatments to control thrip.

Caterpillars

Caterpillars of various types can occasionally pose a problem with ferns. Dipel is an effective natural spray which infects caterpillars (and no other type of animal) with a disease which will kill them without causing any harm to the environment. Pyrethrum sprays are also effective, and relatively safe.

Sciarid flies (Fungus gnats)

Sciarid flies, tiny insects whose adults resemble mosquitoes, can be a real problem for fern growers. The larval stage is a small maggot that generally lives on decaying plant tissue. Some species, however, attack live tissue, particularly on fern prothalli and young ferns. Damage on adult plants is often hard to see above ground; however, infested plants generally lack vigour. A black mould-like or waterlogged surface appearance may be present, particularly with prothalli or young plants. The presence of the small adult flies on or near the soil surface or of small maggots in the soil or potting mix is the best indicator of the problem. Control is best achieved by granular insecticides containing disulfoton. Infected trays of sporelings should be destroyed, unless they are particularly valuable. Some control may be achieved with a carbaryl drench or dip.

Passionvine hoppers

These can be quite troublesome on many ferns, particularly on soft tree ferns *(Dicksonia antarctica)*. They suck the sap from new fronds, causing a lack of vigour and distortion of the frond. The adults are about 7–10 mm long and approximately triangular in shape with clear wings bordered by brown or black markings. The young hoppers are greenish-brown in colour with a tuft of white waxy filaments at the tip of their abdomen. The adult is winged and can fly or jump if disturbed, usually to the underside of the frond, while the young hoppers are wingless but can hop considerable distances at the slightest disturbance. Control can be achieved by the use of pyrethrum or Maldison sprays.

Nematodes

Nematodes (eelworms) are microscopic animals which attack the roots of plants. Most nematodes do not attack ferns, though there are some types which will attack fern foliage, causing wilting, stunting or marking of the fronds. These pests are difficult to control, though the juices from marigold roots will deter them. Chemicals which will kill nematodes are also available, e.g. Fenamiphos.

Millipedes

Millipedes are arthropods with anything up to a few hundred legs. They have two pairs of legs per segment (i.e. 4) and the body can have up to about 100 segments. They are related to centipedes (but centipedes have only one pair of legs per segment).

Millipedes eat vegetation, rotting, dead and living. They can become a garden pest after prolonged rain, especially in greenhouses. They will eat the roots of seedlings and can even cause damage to root vegetables such as potatoes or beetroot.

Some good insecticides will help control millipedes (Carbaryl is the best). Some types of snail baits will have an effect (but not all).

Millipedes breed in moist organic material such as mulch on garden beds. Millipede numbers are reduced if mulch is removed from beds (though this may have some other undesired side effects on the plants).

Diatomaceous earth, often used in swimming pool filters, dusted over the garden may also have some effect in discouraging millipedes.

Red spider mites

Mites are small spiders. Red spider mite is a type of mite found on the undersurface of leaves of a wide range of plants (roses, azaleas, fuchsias, chrysanthemums, vines, etc.).

The adult red spider sucks sap from the veins of leaves. The undersurface of the leaves can become covered with webs, the leaves may become dis-coloured and fall.

Plants which are watered regularly are less susceptible to the mites. Many of the standard pesticides such as white oil and dieldrin do not affect red spider. Systemic insecticides (such as Rogor or Metasystox) are much more effective.

Biocontrol, a company based in Warwick, Queensland, supplies a predatory mite which attacks and kills the red spider mite. This biological control can prove quite successful. The parasitic mite can also be purchased from Hawkesbury Agricultural College on the outskirts of Sydney (Richmond, NSW).

Slaters or woodlice

Slaters (also known as woodlice) are the only crustaceans which live on land. They are, however, dependant on water and tend to be found in dark, damp places. (Other crustaceans include crabs and prawns.)

Slaters eat rotting vegetation and similar material. They can injure the stems and roots of plants and occasionally feed on foliage.

Some snail baits, and some commercial insecticides are effective in killing slaters. A blowtorch or boiling water can also be used to kill them.

Snails and slugs

Snails and slugs are found in moist areas or places sheltered from sun and wind. The tough hard leaves of many Australian natives are not favoured by snails and slugs; they prefer soft juicy foliage. They tend to feed on plant foliage at night and return to protected places through the day.

Snails and slugs can be controlled by snail baits, some of which will break down in the rain; woodshavings, placed around a garden (snails don't like crawling over them); stale beer in a saucer (attracts and eradicates them); the Artemisia species of herb, commonly known as wormwood, is said to deter snails; or by a dusting with diatomaceous earth. Ducks will happily eat snails, though in the process they may damage your plants.

Algae

Algae may be unsightly, but are rarely a serious health problem for established plants. Germinating spores, however, can be affected by algae growing over them. Given that algae is spread, among other things, through tap water, growers are well advised to water spores with sterilised water (boiled), and to keep plants in a sterile environment during the propagation stage.

Damping off

Damping off is a fungal infection which attacks young plants. The result is rot occurring just above soil level, and death. The chemicals Benlate and Terrazole are effective in controlling this problem, though young ferns can be susceptible to chemical burn from them. The best treatment is of course prevention, and the best way to prevent damping off is to maintain good hygiene when propagating young ferns, that is, tools, soil, containers and everything else should be sterile.

Mosses and liverworts

These simple plants flourish in the conditions that are generally preferred by ferns, and they are particularly common in glasshouses. In pots and baskets they can choke out young ferns and prothalli or can smother the surface of the pot so that water runs off the surface and doesn't reach the roots of the ferns. Initial soil sterilisation and good hygiene are the best means of preventing the establishment of mosses and liverworts. If they are established then careful hand removal is the best treatment.

Other fungi

Moulds and other fungal problems can attack both young and established ferns, particularly in conditions of high humidity and poor ventilation. Overcrowding of plants can also lead to fungal problems.

Fungicides such as Fongarid or Benomyl can be useful for control.

Avoiding frost

The vast majority of ferns react poorly to frost. In planning fern plantings, remember there is always a certain amount of protection from frost next to or underneath other structures. Some ferns are highly susceptible to frost and need very good protection to avoid being killed. Others will be burnt by a frost, but rarely killed. Frost hardy plants are not affected at all.

Many plants, not just ferns, are very sensitive when young but once established are frost hardy.
- The tree canopy overhead will usually give protection from slight frosts.
- Frosts are usually worse in low spots—depressions or the bottom of a hill.
- The space which is protected by a wall, fence or some other structure can be roughly calculated as follows: 1. Measure the height of the structure. 2. Measure a distance out from the base of the structure which is equal to half the height of the structure. 3. Take a line from this point (out from the wall) to the top of the structure. Anything growing within the space confined by the wall and the imaginary line should be protected.
- If a plant is burnt by a frost, do not remove the burnt leaves until after the frost period, as they will protect the centre of the plant from further burning.
- If the plant is only frost tender when young then hessian or plastic can be tied to stakes around it for protection until it is past the frost tender age.
- Plant in containers and simply move the plants under cover in the cooler months.

Other environmental problems

A large variety of problems can occur due to detrimental environmental conditions, including salt damage, windburn, smog damage, fog damage,

waterlogging. These problems are generally easily rectified either by moving the plant from the source of the problem or by modifying the effects of the problem. For example, windburn may be prevented by removing the plant to a more protected position or by providing windbreaks; salt problems may be rectified by removing plants to a position where salty soils, water or winds will not affect it, or by leaching salts from soils and potting mixes and providing wind protection against salt-laden winds; waterlogging can be prevented or controlled by improving drainage or by removing the plant to a position with better drainage.

Safety procedures when using agricultural chemicals

Golden Rules for using chemicals

1. *Only use chemicals* when actually needed.
2. Use the correct chemical for the job at hand; if unsure, seek advice.
3. Always read the label, *and* the product information sheets (if supplied).
4. Use protective clothing at *all* times.
5. Use the correct pesticide application equipment.
6. Don't spray on windy or very hot days.
7. Warn other people in the area that you are going to spray (and have sprayed).
8. Wash out all spray equipment thoroughly when finished.
9. Do not eat or smoke while spraying.
10. Wash all protective clothing thoroughly after spraying.
11. Wash yourself thoroughly after spraying—especially the hands.
12. Store spray equipment and chemicals in a safe, locked place.
13. Dispose of empty pesticide containers according to the label instructions.
14. Record all details of spraying.

Using chemicals in greenhouses

Applying pesticides in greenhouses presents special problems. In normal greenhouse operations one works inside the greenhouse. Space is often limited and personal contact with plants and other treated surfaces is almost a certainty. Unauthorised persons should not be allowed in. Ventilation is often kept to a minimum to help maintain temperatures, but as a result, fumes, mists, vapours and dusts may remain in the air for considerable periods.

Certain precautions should be followed to avoid problems when spraying in greenhouses.

- Use full safety equipment including respirators or gas masks, and full waterproof clothing.

- Put up warning signs on the outside of the greenhouse at all entrances.
- Do not enter the building without a face mask unless it has been fully aired for the length of time recommended on the chemical container label.
- All possible skin contact with treated plants should be avoided to minimise absorption of dangerous chemicals or skin irritants.
- Spray at a time of the week when it will generally be possible to avoid entering the greenhouse for a day or two afterwards.

5 Propagation

Propagating ferns can be one of the most enjoyable and addictive activities you may ever embark upon. Ferns can be propagated either by spores or by vegetative techniques, depending on the variety. Generally spore propagation is the simplest method and the most economical way of producing large numbers of new plants quickly. A few varieties will only propagate by vegetative means. In other instances, vegetative propagation is preferred to spore propagation for one of a number of reasons, outlined later in this chapter.

Spore propagation

Spore is generally produced as a result of two plants crossbreeding with each other, although many plants may self-fertilise. Plants grown as a result of crossbreeding may display a mixture of characteristics from the two parents, that is, they do not necessarily turn out like the plant which the spore originally came from, or in the case of self-fertilisation, different combinations of chromosomes from the same parent produce differing characteristics in the offspring, although the differences are generally not as great as those produced by crossbreeding.

Almost all ferns can be propagated from spores which are produced on the underside of fertile fronds. Spores are produced in large quantities and appear to the naked eye like brown dust.

Vegetative propagation

In vegetative propagation a piece of an existing plant is treated in some way to cause the development of roots and top growth, thus producing a new plant. As there is only one parent, the new plant will have all of the same characteristics found in the parent plant.

Ferns can be propagated vegetatively by division, from bulbils, tissue culture, layering or cuttings.

Division

Creeping rhizomes
Ferns with creeping rhizomes can normally be propagated by division. The chance of survival is determined by the presence of roots (sections without roots are difficult to establish), and by the size of the section (very small divisions can be difficult to establish).

Ferns which can be propagated this way include *Pteris* species (the brakes), *Davallia* species (haresfoot ferns) and some of the *Adiantum* species (maidenhairs). Some fishbone ferns (e.g. *Nephrolepis exalatum*) produce small plants on the ends of wiry creeping stems and can readily be propagated by division.

Aerial rhizomes
Ferns such as *Davallia* and some *Phlebodium* species produce a mass of rhizomes which bear roots at their base, and leaves on rootless sections, in the

air. Sections taken must have some roots attached if they are to grow. These are best taken in spring or early summer.

Crown division

Many ferns (e.g. several species of *Polystichum*) form a tufted rhizome at ground level. These tufted 'crowns' over a period can divide over and over, eventually producing a large clump. Crowns can be cut apart with a knife to produce several distinct plants. Roots and fronds on these divisions should be trimmed before potting.

Platycerium division

The stag and elk fern group *(Platycerium)* are usually clump-forming epiphytic ferns with a creeping network of rhizomes behind layers of leaves (called pads). Over time the old leaves die and new layers of leaves grow over them. Divide as follows:
1. Use a sharp knife to cut off a section of a clump. The section must contain some rhizomes, some living leaf and some of the dead pads. Larger divisions are much easier to establish than small ones.
2. Tie the cut section onto a piece of treefern trunk or weathered hardwood, with a few handfuls of moist sphagnum moss in between. Copper wire or nylon fishing line are ideal to tie the fern on.

Early summer is normally the best time to divide these ferns.

Bulbils

Some ferns produce small new plants called 'bulbils' on their fronds. The bulbil has three stages in its formation—it begins with a small ball-like swelling, without leaves or roots, then small fronds start to grow from the swelling, and as the fronds grow larger roots begin to form.

There are two types of bulbils, dormant and active.

Dormant bulbils do not develop roots or fronds until they are removed from the frond they are forming on. In nature dormant bulbils fall off when mature, and begin to grow. Growth can be very slow unless conditions are suitable. *Tectaria gemmifera* is an example of this type.

Active bulbils develop fronds and roots while they are still attached to the parent plant. These are normally propagated by pegging the bulbils down into the ground or a pot and detaching them from the parent plant at a later stage when they are growing strongly.

If roots and fronds have already begun to develop, the bulbils can be detached and planted into a container. Provided good growing conditions are maintained the new plants will develop well from that point.

Plants which can be grown from active bulbils include *Asplenium bulbiferum, A. paleaceum, Polystichum lentum, P. proliferum, P. setiferum, Woodwardia orientalis* and *W. radicans*.

Tissue culture

Tissue culture is simply growing plants either from single cells, or from small pieces of plant tissue.

Also called 'micropropagation', tissue culture involves multiplying plants under sterile laboratory conditions. Basically, a microscopic section of a plant is placed in a nutrient environment (a jelly impregnated with the nutrients essential to plant growth) and then left in a perfectly disease-free environment where all conditions such as temperature, moisture, light, etc. are controlled. After a period of time the microscopic section of plant will grow. Eventually it can be moved (via a series of stages) into the harsher outside environment.

Many fern species can be propagated successfully by tissue culture, though few are grown on a large scale using this technique. Westland Nurseries in Tasmania use tissue culture to propagate *Nephrolepis* species on a large scale.

Generally micropropagation techniques are beyond the reach of the majority of gardeners in both expertise and the initial high costs of equipment; however, as more research is undertaken in this area it is likely that the technique will fall within reach of many more people.

For people interested in further information on this topic, the Proceedings of the International Plant Propagators Society provide a useful source. In addition the book *'Plants From Test Tubes'* by Kyte (Timber Press) is a useful text. This can be obtained from the Australian Horticultural Correspondence School at 264 Swansea Rd, Lilydale, 3140, which also provides correspondence courses in such areas as Tissue Culture and Fern Growing.

1. Most ferns prefer a situation with filtered sunlight (no direct sun, but a reasonable amount of light). Extremely bright or very dark conditions suit very few varieties

2. Protected by buildings and tall trees, this is an ideal site for most ferns, being shaded and protected from both wind and temperature extremes

3. Fern landscape surrounding pond and waterfall (note the variation in foliage textures, and the contrast of foliage against rock)

4. An attractive corner fernery. *Cyathea cooperi* provides height and forms the main feature surrounded by a range of smaller ferns providing contrast in colour and foliage texture.

5. Fernery featuring old logs as a central feature and base for growing a variety of ferns

6. Simple, inexpensive pond made by lining a hole with several layers of black plastic over a base of fine sand

10. *Asplenium oblongifolium* foliage damaged by insects

7. Mealy bug and sooty mould

8. *Adiantum* damaged by winter cold and other environmental conditions. Warmer weather in spring will cause this semi-deciduous fern to regenerate

9. Scale insects

11. Insect damage on *Asplenium scolopendrium*

12. *Polystichum retroso* spore

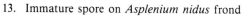

14. Spore on *Polystichum rigens*

15. Bulbils on *Asplenium bulbiferum* fronds

13. Immature spore on *Asplenium nidus* frond

18. Kangaroo Fern *(Phymatosorus diversifolium)* in a wire hanging basket

16. Assorted ferns in a hanging basket

17. *Cyathea cooperi* growing in a tub carved from a section of tree fern trunk

19. Staghorn Fern growing in a wire hanging basket

20. *Adiantum* 'Joyce', a hybrid originating in Tasmania (p.55)

23. *Asplenium aethiopicum* (p.59)

21. *Adiantum wrightii* (p.55)

22. *Alsophila australis*, Rough Tree Fern, also known as *Cyathea australis* (p.56)

24. *Asplenium nidus*, Bird's Nest Fern (p.59)

25. *Asplenium oblongifolium* (p.59)

26. *Asplenium scolopendrium* (p.59)

29. *Blechnum* sp. (p.61)

27. *Athyrium felix-femina grandiceps* (p.60)

28. *Azolla filliculoides* (p.60)

30. *Blechnum cartilagineum* (p.61)

31. *Blechnum contiguum* (p.61)

32. *Blechnum discolor*—note the discolouration on the tip of the frond caused by the production of spore (p.61)

35. *Blechnum minus*—established on road embankment near Foster, Victoria (p.61)

33. *Blechnum discolor* (p.61)

34. *Blechnum fluviatile* (p.61)

36. *Blechnum nudum* (p.61)

37. *Blechnum penna-marina* (p.61)

38. *Blechnum spicant* (p.61)

41. *Campyloneurum angustifolium* (p.62)

39. *Blechnum watsii*, Hard Water Fern (p.61)

40. *Blechnum watsii* hybrid in foreground—note one of the parents behind (p.61)

42. *Cheilanthes* (p.63)

43. *Cyathea* sp.—in fern tub (p.65)

44. *Cyathea brownii* planted in a shadehouse in Gippsland, Victoria; this plant has increased in size more than fourfold in the first year from planting (p.65)

47. *Cyathea marcescens*, Skirted Tree Fern, thought to be a hybrid of *C. cunninghamii* and *C. australis* (p.65)

45. *Cyathea cooperi*, Slender Tree Fern (p.65)

46. *Cyathea cooperi*, Slender Tree Fern (p.65)

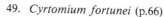

48. *Cyrtomium falcatum*, Holly Fern (p.66)

49. *Cyrtomium fortunei* (p.66)

50. *Davallia* sp. (p.66)

53. *Dryopteris affinis*—spore on frond (p.69)

51. *Dicksonia antarctica* (p.67)

52. *Dryopteris affinis* (p.69)

54. *Dryopteris erythrosora* (p.69)

55. *Dryopteris filix-mas* (p.69)

56. *Gleichenia* sp., Coral Fern (p.69)

58. *Lastreopsis grayii* (p.71)

57. *Hemionitis arifolia* (p.70)

59. *Lindsaea* sp., Climbing Fern (p.72)

60. *Nephrolepis cordifolia*, Fishbone Fern (p.75)

61. *Nephrolepis exalata* 'Bostoiensis' (p.75)

62. *Marsilea drummondii*, Nardoo, Water Fern (p.74)

63. *Osmunda regalis* (p.77)

64. *Pellaea rotundifolia* (p.77)

65. *Phyllitis scolopendrium* (p.78)

66. *Phymatosorus diversifolium*, Kangaroo Fern, growing as an epiphyte on a tree fern trunk (p.78)

67. *Platycerium bifurcatum* (p.79)

68. *Platycerium superbum*, Staghorn Fern (p.79)

71. *Polystichum proliferum* (p.80)

69. *Polypodium subauriculatum knightiae* (p.80)

70. *Polypodium vulgare* (p.80)

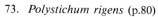

72. *Polystichum retroso* (p.80)

73. *Polystichum rigens* (p.80)

74. *Psilotum* sp.

75. *Pyrrosia lingua* (p.81)

76. *Sadleria cyatheoides* (p.82)

77. *Sticherus tener* (p.83)

78. *Todea barbara* (p.84)

79. *Woodwardia orientalis* (p.85)

80. Ferns growing under glass in the Munich Botanic Gardens, Germany

81. Timber slat Fern House, Ballarat Botanic Gardens, Victoria

82. Entrance to Fern Gullies at the Rhododendron Garden, Olinda, Victoria. Note the contrast in texture between the tree ferns and other plants

83. Fern Gully at Pirianda Gardens in the Dandenong Ranges, Melbourne

Layering

Layering involves either pinning part of a plant down into soil, which induces new plants to grow from the part pinned down, or placing sphagnum moss around part of a plant to induce root growth into the sphagnum (aerial layering). The layered section, once growing well, can be detached from the parent plant to give a new plant.

Aerial layering

Davallia rhizomes may be aerially layered:
1. Place a small handful of moist sphagnum or peat moss around part of an aerial rhizome.
2. Wrap a sheet of clear plastic firmly around the handful of moss and tie with string at the top and bottom.
3. Within three months you should be able to see roots growing under the plastic. At this point cut the rooted section off, remove the plastic and plant into a container.

Layering of proliferous frond tips

In some ferns, e.g. *Asplenium caudatum*, the tip of the frond grows an elongated section which on contact with soil will sprout roots and fronds to produce a new growth. Once vigorous growth is established, the new plant can be removed and potted.

Offsets

Some species of tree fern produce sideshoots from the base which when cut off and planted can grow into new plants. *Cyathea rebeccae, Dicksonia youngiae* and *Dicksonia squarrosa* can all be propagated in this way.

Spore propagation

The quality of the spore is the most important factor in spore propagation. Spore which is immature or too old will not grow. Unless your source of spore is reliable, you are well advised to collect your own.

Spore occurs in clumps or patches (called *sori*) on the underside of fertile fronds. Not all fronds will bear spore and for each species of fern spore only occurs at a set time of the year. The clumps or sori are, for each fern species, arranged in a pattern unique to that species. The arrangement of the sori is often used by botanists in identification of ferns, e.g. in *Adiantum* sori occur on the margins of the pinnae, while in other ferns they occur on the veins or midribs.

Collecting spore

As spore reaches maturity it changes colour, usually turning brown. Once mature it becomes loose and begins to drop from the frond. The fern must be watched closely around this time to determine the best time to collect the spore. A magnifying glass can be very useful to more closely examine the changes occurring. Check to see whether spores are becoming loose, but that there is still spore there to collect.

Spore from *Todea, Osmunda* and *Leptopteris* are green when mature. Spore from *Dicksonia* and *Polypodium* are yellow when ripe. Spore from most other species are brown or occasionally black when ripe.

The easiest way to collect spore is to remove the fronds you wish to collect spore from and put them in white paper bags. If left in a warm place (approx. 20–25°C) for a few days, the spore will drop from the frond. Spore can then be stored in an airtight container placed in a cool dry place. The spore of some fern species must be sown fresh and will not keep in storage at all, while the length of time you can store others varies.

Equipment and materials

To germinate well, spore needs a clean environment free of disease, algae, insects, etc.; a wet environment (very moist and humid, never becoming dry); and for most species a temperature around 18 to 22°C.

Almost any container can be used as long as it is sterilised (plant pots, old plastic takeaway food containers, nursery trays, etc). Wash all containers before use with hot water and soap, then soak for 15 minutes in a solution of sodium hypochlorite, Biogram, formalin or Dettol. You should also give this treatment to anything which the container or spore will come in contact with—tools and work benches, etc.

The container must be filled with a medium (propagating mix) which is both clean and has the ability to retain water. Suitable mixes include:

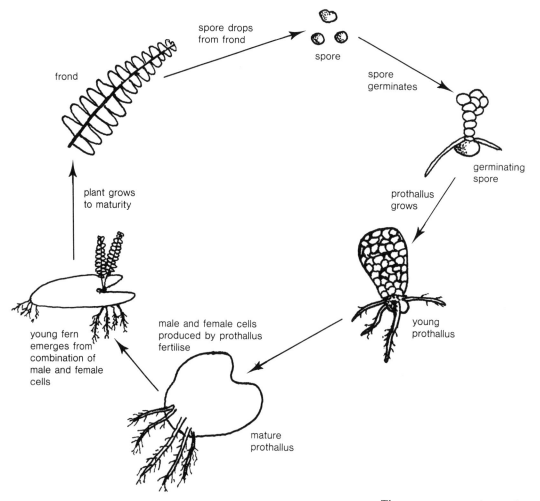

The spore propagation cycle

1 part vermiculite to 3 parts peat moss
1 part perlite to 2 parts peat moss
Sieved sphagnum moss
1 part sphagnum moss to 1 part crushed
terracotta pots
A commercially prepared orchid potting mix

N.B. Do not buy the cheapest materials—they are
the most likely to be contaminated with disease.
Remember, you get what you pay for.

During the propagation stage the water used to
water the spore should be boiled before use to kill
algae or other contaminants. (Be sure the water has
cooled before using it!) It is advantageous to apply
water which is as close as possible to the ideal
germinating temperature, about 20°C.

Sowing spore

1. Fill the container with fern propagating mix,
keeping it about 5 mm below the top of the
container.
2. Even out the surface and water well. If you have
to use a container with no drainage holes, be careful
not to overwater.
3. Sow the spore very carefully. A common cause
of failure is sowing spore too thickly. To prevent this,
a good technique is to place a small amount of spore
on the tip of a knife blade and gently tap the blade
to release the spore as you move it over the surface.
Another method is to mix some spore with fine dry
sand (*very* dry sand), then sow the mixture to get
a more even covering.
4. Place a sheet of clear plastic (Clingwrap or

Gladwrap), or a sheet of glass over the top of the container.

5. Put the container in a place which will provide the preferred temperature conditions for germination. Over winter this may be in a greenhouse, though a greenhouse may at times be too warm for some species to grow. It is important that the containers also receive ample light. For some species, the use of a hotbed to heat the bottom of the container may be helpful.

6. If watering is necessary while spore is developing, it is best done using a fine mist sprayer.

What happens next

As the spores germinate they grow a moss-like covering over the surface of the propagating medium. This covering will after a few months sprout leaves and grow roots at points throughout the medium to produce new fern plants.

Potting up the small plants

Once two or three fronds have appeared, the young ferns can be carefully removed with a knife and planted into a small pot or tub. They should be placed either under a misting system in a hot house or in a humid coldframe for about a month, then moved to a less pampered environment to harden off.

6 Growing Ferns in Containers

Most ferns will grow successfully in containers provided the containers are placed in an environment suited to that variety. Some varieties, particularly those with sensitive root systems, are not suited to growing in containers at all.

There are a number of points to remember when choosing ferns to grow in containers. Firstly, there is a greater tendency for temperature to fluctuate in the root zone of a container-grown plant. The roots will almost certainly get hotter on a hot day and colder over a cold night than they would if planted in the ground. Secondly, the roots are restricted to the volume of the container. A vigorous fern cannot invade and compete for nourishment with neighbouring plants. Thirdly, a container has only a limited supply of nutrients. When you water a container nutrients are leached through and lost. Feeding is thus more important for container plants than those growing in the ground. Lastly, plants in containers tend to dry out faster than those growing in the ground.

Baskets

There are basically two types of hanging basket, the open framework of wire, timber or some other material which needs to be lined with sphagnum moss or bark (usually from a melaleuca) to retain the soil, and the solid basket with small holes for drainage. These solid types should have a little better than average drainage material in the bottom, e.g. crocks (broken pieces of ceramic material) or stones.

Ferns in hanging baskets are more exposed, thus they dry out faster. Plants which can withstand periods of dryness are ideal for baskets, e.g. Nephrolepis. Almost any plant can be grown in a basket, though some will require a lot more attention than others. Baskets can be grown inside or outside—depending on the type of plant used.

Epiphytes

Epiphytes are plants which can grow on other plants. Stag or elk ferns which grow on the trunk or limbs of large trees are well-known examples. Most epiphytes will grow attached to a living plant, a piece of wood (which can be hung on a wall), a slab of some other type of material (provided there is ample organic matter behind the plant for it to feed on) or alternatively in a container (but the growing medium needs to be very rich in organic matter). Some epiphytic ferns will grow equally well as an epiphyte or in normal soil. Epiphytic ferns can be fed by tucking organic material such as fruit or vegetable scraps behind or under the fronds.

Various epiphytic ferns growing on tree fern trunk slabs

Terrariums

Terrariums, plants growing inside enclosed transparent containers, may be established in bottles, jars, glass domes or other such things. Terrariums have many advantages. To a large extent, they insulate from the outside environment, protecting plants from periods of low temperature and low humidity which can be a problem for many ferns. They also protect plants from draughts of cold air. There are, however, disadvantages to growing ferns in terrariums. Disease can develop more easily and plants can easily become too hot in a terrarium. Never place a terrarium in direct sunlight. Problems with terrariums are generally more likely if the container is sealed—an uncorked bottle or an old aquarium with the lid left off will be less likely to have problems with disease or heat build up.

There are many different ways of providing soil in the bottom of a terrarium. Often a thin layer of charcoal chunks is placed at the bottom to help with drainage. (Excess water sitting in charcoal is less likely to breed disease.) On top of this, sometimes a thin layer of sand or sphagnum moss is used before a layer of potting mix. Sometimes the potting mix is placed straight on top of the charcoal. The potting mix can be any standard fern potting mix, provided it is well drained and high in organic matter.

After placing the soil medium into the terrarium container, you can plant it and water it. Remember, though, watering should be sparse for a terrarium. There is nowhere for excess water to go, and that makes the problem of overwatering something you must watch very carefully.

A very simple terrarium can be made from an empty 2-litre softdrink bottle. The black cup stuck to the base of the bottle is simply pulled off. The top neck section can be cut off and the bottle inverted, then fitted into the base cup to make a domed cover. There are holes in the base for the plant to drain, but a hole about 1.25 cm across should be cut in the top for ventilation. Soil can be put in the black cup and plants planted there, e.g. wandering jew, moss, peperomia, african violet and ivy, then the bottle dome fitted on top.

Pots and tubs

Growing ferns in tubs or other containers has certain advantages and disadvantages. Above all, plants in tubs are flexible—they make a landscape changeable. Tub plants can be removed out of view when they are sick and returned when they become healthy again. Plants in tubs need more watering and feeding than those in soil, so it is essential that the tub be properly drained. Sufficient holes in the bottom of the tub are needed, and perhaps some large stones for a layer below the soil.

Other containers

Nonglazed ceramic containers will drain through the water-absorbent walls and generally require a soil mix which retains more moisture. Glazed ceramics and plastics absorb no moisture at all though the sides of the pot, thus needing more holes in the bottom, and a potting mix which has very good drainage characteristics.

Timber containers will rot after a time if not treated regularly with some type of timber preservative such as creosote. Remember that treated pine does not necessarily last for years.

Maintaining plants in pots

During warmer months it can be advantageous to mulch the surface of the pots to prevent water loss. In windy or hot weather, pots of ferns should be kept in a protected position, as either wind or sunlight can speed up the rate of water loss considerably. This is more critical for porous ceramics such as terracotta.

If you are going away during warm weather, you can prolong the period potted plants don't need watering by sitting the container in a bucket or pond containing water. The water should not cover more than the bottom quarter of the roots though. This treatment is not a preferred way to treat ferns and should not be done for prolonged periods.

Most ferns growing in containers should be potted up every few years. This is necessary to maintain the health of the fern.

The few ferns which are particularly susceptible to root disturbance you should avoid potting up. If a fern remains in a pot for too many years, its roots can become congested. The tight rootball may repel water so that when you water the plant the water runs down between the side of the pot and the outer edge of the roots without properly wetting the roots in the centre. A plant which has reached this stage has probably depleted most of its nutrients and become susceptible to attack by pests and diseases due to a general low level of health.

When you pot up a plant, remove some of the old roots and soil. If the plant is very potbound you will need to break up the old root ball a lot. You can repot it back into the same container it came from, provided around 25% or more of the old soil and roots have been removed and replaced with fresh potting mix. If you pot into a larger container, you might not need to remove so much of the old soil and roots.

PART B

Directory of Ferns in Cultivation

In this directory the ferns are listed alphabetically by genera. Following the genus name is the common name for that group, if they have one, and the family that particular genus belongs to. More than one family may be listed, as fern classification is very confusing, with family names varying according to which classification system you follow.

Acrostichum (Swamp Fern)
Pteridaceae or Polypodiaceae

At a glance
Number of species: 3 (2 Australian)
Natural habitat: Coastal mangrove swamps in tropics.
Hardiness: Hardy in warm climates.
Habit: Large tall clumps with creeping hollow rhizomes.
Growth rate: Slow.
Fronds: Leaves thick or leathery, pinnate and to 1 m long.

Culture
• Grown under glass in temperate climates.
• Does not like roots to be disturbed—avoid cultivation or transplanting.

Varieties
A. aureum (Leather Fern): 1–3 m tall, pantropical.

A. crinitum (Elephant Ear Fern): Leaves to 0.7 m long; also known as *Elaphoglossum crinitum.*
A. daneifolium (Leather Fern): Clump 2–4 m tall, tropical; also known as *A. excelsum.*

Actiniopteris (Radiating Fern)

At a glance
Number of species: 5.
Natural habitat: Dry, arid rocky areas, Africa to India.
Hardiness: Hardy.
Habit: Tuft-forming.
Fronds: Similar to palm fronds.

Culture
• Requires a coarse well drained soil.
• Preferably grown in small pots.
• Water well when putting on growth.
• Water sparingly during dormant periods.

Adiantum (Maidenhair Fern) — Plates 20, 21
Adiantaceae or Polypodiaceae

At a glance
Number of species: Over 200.
Natural habitat: Mainly tropical, some temperate; moist positions, often sunny, sometimes shaded.

Hardiness: Hardy (but can die in extreme conditions).
Habit: Small clumps, often spreading.
Growth rate: In ideal conditions, rapid.
Fronds: Thin, delicate, simple or divided into fan-shaped pinnules. Small up to 1 m long black or brown leaf stalks.

Culture
• Tropical species require 18–22°C and humid environment.
• Varies greatly according to variety.
• Most need frequent watering over summer but little water over winter.
• Respond to small doses of fertiliser regularly.
• Some are very heavy feeders.
• Potting mix should be well drained, and its pH should not drop too low.
• Problems can include snails, caterpillars, aphids, earwigs and botrytis.
• Spores germinate best at a pH between 7 and 8.5.

Varieties

Species	Common name	Height	Fronds
A. aethiopicum	Common Maidenhair	to 0.8 m	3-4 pinnate
A. anceps	Two-edged Maidenhair	0.5 to 1 m	2 pinnate
A. capillus-junonis		to 0.3 m	1 pinnate
A. capillus-veneris	European Maidenhair	0.3 to 0.6 m	2-3 pinnate
A. caudatum	Trailing Maidenhair	0.2 m	1 pinnate
A. cunninghamii	Large Maidenhair	to 1 m	2-3 pinnate
A. diaphanum	Filmy Maidenhair	to 0.3 m	1-2 pinnate
A. hispidulum	Rough Maidenhair	to 0.5 m	2-3 pinnate
A. formosum	Giant Maidenhair	to 1.5 m	3-4 pinnate
A. pedatum	Five Finger Fern	to 0.5 m	2-3 pinnate
A. peruvianum	Silver Dollar Fern	to 1 m	2 pinnate
A. raddianum		0.1 to 0.6 m	2-3 pinnate
A. tenerum		to 0.8 m	3-5 pinnate

There are many varieties of A. pedatum, A. raddianum, A. tenerum and A. capillus-veneris available.

Aglaomorpha
Polypodiaceae

At a glance
Number of species: Approximately 10.
Natural habitat: Generally tropical wet climates.
Hardiness: Medium.
Habit: Large epiphytes; thick scale-covered rhizomes.
Fronds: Leathery, glabrous, deeply pinnatifid, up to 2 m long.

Culture
• Grow outdoors in tropics.
• Greenhouse plant in temperate regions with some heating.
• Grow well in hanging baskets.
• Propagate by spores or division.

Varieties

Plant	Common name	Leaves	General
A. coroans		0.7-1.5 m long	From subtropics
A. heracleum		1-2 m	From tropics
A. meyeniana	Bear's Paw	0.7-1 m	From Philippines

Aleuritopteris
Frequently known as *Cheilanthes*.

Allantodia
Changed to *Diplazium* over 150 years ago.

Alsophila (Tree Fern) — Plate 22
Cyatheaceae

At a glance
Number of species: Approximately 200.
Natural habitat: Mainly tropical, some temperate to Tasmania and New Zealand.
Hardiness: Varies; many are hardy.
Habit: Tree ferns.
Growth rate: Varies.
Fronds: 2-3 pinnate, large.
Comments: Sometimes included in *Cyathea*.

Culture
• As for Cyathea.
• Some species grown outdoors both in ground and as tub plants.
• Propagate from spores.

Varieties

Species	Height	Leaf length	Origin	Climate
A. australis	to 6 m	to 4 m	Australia	Needs protection in warmer climates, otherwise hardy
N.B. Cyathea australis = A. australis				
A. cunninghamii	to 6 m	to 1.5 m	Australia/ New Zealand	Shaded, moist soils, needs protection
A. dregei	to 1.2 m	to 3 m	South Africa	Shade and moist soils
A. smithii	to 5 m	to 3 m	New Zealand	Cold, moist
A. tricolor	to 10 m	to 2.5 m	New Zealand	Moist soil

Ampelopteris

Polypodiaceae or Thelypteridaceae

At a glance
Number of species: 1.
Natural habitat: South-East Asia to Queensland.
Hardiness: Frost tender.
Habit: Long creeping fleshy rhizomes.
Growth rate: Fast.
Fronds: Very long with small plantlets at the axis of some pinnae.
Comments: Often spreads to form large clumps.

Culture
• Grows readily in a protected position.
• Needs a warm climate.
• Adapts to a variety of soils.
• Frost tender.

Varieties
A. prolifera is the only species.

Amphineuron

Thelypteridaceae or Polypodiaceae

At a glance
Number of species: 10 (1 Australian).
Natural habitat: Generally tropical, South-East Asia, New Guinea and Australia.
Hardiness: Hardy.
Habit: Tuft-forming; upright or creeping rhizomes.
Growth rate: Moderate.
Fronds: Bipinnatifid and large.
Comments: Formerly included in the genus *Cyclosorus*.

Culture
• Prefers sheltered, moist positions.
• Generally easy to grow.
• Grows well in large pots.
• Is cold sensitive.

Anarthropteris

Polypodiaceae

At a glance
Number of species: 1.
Natural habitat: New Zealand forests (mainly North Island), on trees, rocks or rotting logs.
Hardiness: Hardy, once established.

Habit: Epiphytic; tufts emerge from long rhizomes.
Growth rate: Slow at first, then can be quite fast.
Fronds: Long, lance-shaped, dark green once established.

Culture
• Needs humid conditions with reasonable air circulation.
• Best in coarse, mostly organic potting mixes (e.g. containing lots of chunky, composted bark).

Anemia (Flowering Fern)

Schizaeaceae

At a glance
Number of species: Approximately 90.
Natural habitat: Tropical, moist, mainly from America but some eleswhere.
Hardiness: Generally hardy, but needs protection in cooler climates.
Habit: Terrestial, upright, small to medium size.
Fronds: Leathery and tough.

Culture
• Prefers well drained soils.
• Needs shelter from extremes of temperature.

Varieties

Species	Common name	Height	General
A. adiantifolia	Pine Fern	to 1 m	Requires warm conditions
A. phyllitidis		to 0.7 m	Requires warm moist conditions
A. mexicana	Holly Fern		Hardy, most commonly grown type
A. rotundifolia		to 0.4 m	Requires warm moist conditions

Angiopteris (Turnip Fern)

Marattiaceae

At a glance
Number of species: Approximately 100.
Natural habitat: Madagascar, Australia, Southern Japan and Polynesia; wet forests, commonly alongside rivers and streams.
Hardiness: Very hardy if kept wet.
Habit: Terrestrial, very large.
Growth rate: Slow to moderate.
Fronds: Massive fronds up to 4 or 5 m long, pinnae up to 50 cm long.

Culture
- In tropical greenhouses.
- Propagate by spores.
- Very wet.
- Cool humid position—never cold.

Varieties
Even though there are many species, they are often grouped together by botanists into the single species *A. evecta*.

A. evecta (King Fern): From the rainforests of north-east Queensland; has been grown as far south as Melbourne if protected.

Anisogonium
Included in *Diplazium*.

Anissorus
Included in *Lonchitis*.

Anogramma
Adiantaceae or Hemionitidaceae

At a glance
Number of species: Approximately 7 (1 Australian).
Natural habitat: Warm climates, along shaded watercourses.
Hardiness: Generally delicate to moderately hardy.
Habit: Small annual ferns growing from a perennial prothallus. Fresh fertile fronds appear in cooler wetter months to spring and die back over summer.
Growth rate: Fast in the right conditions.
Fronds: Small delicate bipinnate to tripinnate, often brittle.

Culture
- Hot, dry conditions will cause dieback to the roots.
- Moist soil.
- Shaded position.

Anopteris
Polypodiaceae

At a glance
Number of species: 1.
Natural habitat: West Indies, the Greater Antilles, warm climates; on limestone soils, particularly on cliff faces.

Hardiness: Moderately hardy.
Habit: Small, terrestrial, clump-forming.
Growth rate: Medium to fast.
Fronds: Variable, up to 60 cm, usually smaller, 2–4 pinnate, often dimorphic, fertile pinnules normally narrower.
Comments: 2 subspecies are recognised, one with finely divided fronds, the other with coarse fronds.

Culture
- Warm, humid conditions.
- Coarse, open soil preferred.
- pH should be alkaline or neutral—never acid.

Antrophyum
Vittariaceae

At a glance
Number of species: Approximately 40 (3 in Australia).
Natural habitat: Tropics.
Hardiness: Hardy once established.
Habit: Epiphytes, mainly on boulders or rocky outcrops, sometimes on trees.
Growth rate: Slow.
Fronds: Fleshy or leathery, simple, often tongue-shaped, weeping.

Culture
- Very difficult to establish.
- Must have high humidity.
- Grown on slabs or in pots filled with high organic potting mix.
- Suitable for hanging baskets.

Apteropteris (Filmy Fern)
Hymenophyllaceae

At a glance
Number of species: 2 (1 Tasmania, 1 New Zealand).
Natural habitat: Cool rainforests.
Hardiness: Difficult to cultivate.
Habit: Forms mats on logs, tree trunks or rocks; fine branching rhizomes, small, semi-erect to weeping forms.
Growth rate: Slow.
Fronds: Fronds to 20 cm long covered with small hairs.
Comments: Often included in the genus *Hymenophyllum*.

Culture

- Needs moist humid conditions.
- Needs partial shade.
- Needs temperate constant temperature.

Arachniodes
Aspidiceae or Polypodiaceae

At a glance
Number of species: Approximately 20 to 50 (authorities vary).
Natural habitat: Warm climates—Asia and Polynesia.
Hardiness: Cultivated varieties are hardy.
Habit: Creeping, long rhizomes.
Growth rate: Variable according to variety.
Fronds: Thick leaves 0.3–0.8 m long, glossy green.
Comments: Has been at times included in *Polystichum*.

Culture

- Needs moist well drained soils.
- Easily grown in pots or protected positions.

Varieties

Species	Common name	Fronds	General
A. aristata	East Indian Holly Fern	Ovate-triangular, glabrous or variegated	1 m high, attractive, dark green fronds
A. hasseltii		Triangular shape, 3-pinnate	Needs protection in cool climates
A. simplicior	Variegated Shield Fern	Bright green, yellow variegation	Needs protection, slow growing
A. standishii	Upside Down Fern	Ovate-triangular, glabrous	Fast growing; greenhouse best in temperate climates

Araiostegia
Davalliaceae or Polypodiaceae

At a glance
Number of species: 12.
Natural habitat: Tropical to cool mountain situations, India, Taiwan and South-East Asia.
Hardiness: Varies between varieties.
Habit: Epiphytic and terrestrial; large fleshy rhizomes with scales.
Fronds: Fine, thin, dissected, sometimes deciduous.
Comments: Closely related to Davallia.

Culture

- Tropical species need a heated greenhouse in cooler climates.
- Cool climate varieties need open well drained mixes.
- Grow well in containers or baskets.
- Drainage is essential.
- Most need light but not direct sun—well lit shaded position is ideal.
- Grow best in warmth and high humidity.
- Generally frost tender but otherwise will survive in cool climates.
- Can be deciduous.

Varieties

Species	Height	Fronds	Habit	General
A. hymenophylloides	1 m	4–5 pinnate	Epiphytic	Needs warmth and humidity
A. pseudocystopteris	0.6 m	3–4 pinnate	Epiphytic or terrestrial	Grows in cooler climates
A. pulchra	0.5 m	2–3 pinnate	Epiphytic	Needs shade and can be deciduous

Arthropteris
Oleandraceae or Nephrolepidaceae

At a glance
Number of species: Approximately 20 (4 Australian).
Natural habitat: Tropical and temperate wet sites.
Hardiness: Hardy once established.
Habit: Small epiphytes and rock ferns, with long thin rhizomes; form matted clumps or grow like climbers.
Growth rate: Good once established.
Fronds: Delicate, small to medium size.
Comments: Related to *Nephrolepis*.

Culture

- Cool humid sites.
- Needs moisture.
- Good in tree fern baskets.
- Can be difficult to establish.

Varieties

Species	Height	Fronds	Habit
A. beckleri	0.2 m	Upright or weeping, dull green	Forms mats on rocks
A. palisotti	0.4 m	Shiny green, upright or weeping	Forms thick mats mainly on trees—sometimes on rocks

Asplenium (Spleenwort) — Plates 23–26
Aspleniaceae or Polypodiaceae

At a glance

Number of species: Approximately 700.
Natural habitat: Greatly varied.
Hardiness: Many very hardy.
Habit: Clump forming, size varies; can be epiphytes, terrestrial or rock dwellers.
Growth rate: Generally fast.
Fronds: Usually simple deeply cut leaves, or compound. Frond shape can vary according to growing conditions.

Culture

• Avoid direct sun under glass.
• Excess moisture can cause yellowing in periods of slow growth.
• Mainly propagated by spore (but spore must be fresh).
• A few are propagated by division.
• Some can be propagated from bulbils.
• Hybrids are common.

Varieties

Species	Fronds	Height	Comments
A. australasicum	Long, broad	to 0.5 m	Does not like overwatering
A. belangeri	Long, narrow	to 0.5 m	Snails can be a problem
A. bradleyi	Oblong to lanceolate		
A. bulbiferum	2–3 pinnate	1.2 m	Bulblets form on tips of leaves
A. daucifolium	3–4 pinnate	to 0.6 m	Bulblets form on tips
A. falcatum	1–2 pinnate	to 1 m	Also known as A. polyodon
A. flaccidum	2 pinnate	to 1 m	Excellent hanging basket specimen
A. ebenoides	1 pinnate	to 0.5 m	A hybrid of A. platyneuron
A. flabellifolium	1 pinnate, pale green	0.3 m	Necklace Fern, normally a drooping habit
A. hookerianum	1–2 pinnate	0.2 m	Very cold resistant
A. incisum	1–2 pinnate	0.3 m	Needs acidic soil
A. nidus	Simple	2 m	Birdsnest fern
A. oblongifolium	1 pinnate	1.2 m	Likes filtered sun
A. obtusatum	1 pinnate, fleshy	0.3 m	Grows on coast among rocks
A. pinnatifidum	Pinnatifid	0.1 m	Easy to grow
A. ruta-muraria	2–3 pinnate	0.1 m	Wall Spleenwort
A. scolopendrium	Entire	0.2–0.5 m	Many varieties available
A. serratum	Entire	to 0.5 m	American Birdsnest Fern
A. trichomanes	1 pinnate	0.2 m	Common Spleenwort
A. viride	1 pinnate	0.1 m	Needs alkaline soil

Asplenosorus

Hybrids between Asplenium and Camptosorus. Some authorities now include these hybrids in the Asplenium genus.

Athyrium — Plate 27
Athyriaceae

At a glance

Number of species: Approximately 25 (100 by some authorities)
Natural habitat: Mainly subtropical forests to open grasslands; some even from alpine areas.
Hardiness: Generally hardy.
Habit: Mainly terrestrial.
Growth rate: Normally fast.
Fronds: Finely divided, often brittle.
Comments: Sometimes included in the genus *Asplenium*.

Culture

• Propagate from spores.
• Often deciduous in winter.

Varieties

Species	Fronds	General
A. alpestre	to 1 m long	From cold climates, North America; short rhizomes
A. filix-femina	to 1.5 m long	Lady Fern. Hardy, from temperate climate, many varieties available
A. georingianum	to 0.5 m long	Drooping, deciduous leaves, hardy, from Japan
A. niponicum var. pictum	Small	Japanese Painted Fern. Deciduous, grey-green fronds with silver variegation, needs good drainage, hardy in cool climates

Azolla (Water Fern) — Plate 28
Salviniaceae

At a glance

Number of species: 6.
Natural habitat: Aquatic, mainly warm climates.
Hardiness: Hardy, sometimes a weed.
Habit: Float freely on the surface of water.
Growth rate: Very fast.
Fronds: Can turn reddish in full sun; moss-like growth.
Comments: Lives in symbiotic relationship with blue-green algae (called *Anabaera azolla*).

Culture

• Will grow in mild temperate climates.
• Grown as a water plant in ornamental ponds.
• Don't grow in fresh water (fresh water does not have the algae required for symbiosis).
• Propagates readily by division.

Varieties

Species	Fronds	General
A. caroliniana	Green, reddish in full sun	Common in America and West Indies, needs bright sunlight
A. filiculoides	Frequently reddish; fragments easily	Most common in Australia and New Zealand; hardy and easily grown
A. pinnata	Moss-like, free floating	Common in Australia, not New Zealand; not so hardy in the cold

Belvisia
Polypodiaceae

At a glance
Number of species: Approximately 25 (1 Australian).
Natural habitat: Africa, South-East Asia and the Pacific.
Hardiness: Hardy.
Habit: Clump-forming.
Growth rate: Slow.
Fronds: Long strap-like fronds with a tail-like long narrow tip.

Culture
• Easy to grow.
• Needs good drainage.
• Best in greenhouses.
• Slaters and earwigs are a common soil problem.
• Aphis and caterpillars can be a problem.
• pH can be significant when germinating spores.

Varieties
B. mucronata: Grows 0.3 to 0.6 m, with distinctive stag-like fronds, with a long tail at the end of each fertile frond.

Blechnum (Water Ferns) — Plates 29–40
Polypodiaceae or Blechnaceae

At a glance
Number of species: Over 200 (approximately 35 in Australia).
Natural habitat: Dry air, moist roots, widespread throughout the world. More are tropical than temperate.
Hardiness: Hardy.
Habit: Clump-forming, some with rhizomes, most are terrestrial; rhizome covered with shiny narrow scales.
Growth rate: Varies between species.

Fronds: New growth on some is attractively coloured, normally pinnate, resembling the fronds of fishbone, but can be lobed or divided.

Culture
• Most are easy to cultivate.
• Ideally 18–22°C.
• Prefer shade.
• Dry atmosphere and moist root zone.
• Suited to growing in containers.
• Normally propagated by spores.
• Some rhizome types propagated by division.

Varieties

Species	Height	Common name	Hardiness	General
B. articulatum	0.5-1 m	Rosy Water Fern	Hardy	Slow growing, needs mulching
B. brasiliense	0.5-2 m	Brazilian Tree Fern	Very	Large trunk forming
B. capense	to 3 m	Palm Leaf Fern	Very	Needs wet acid soil
B. cartilagineum	1.5 m	Gristle Fern	Very	Young growth bronze
B. discolor	to 1 m	Crown Fern	Very	Needs wet soil, shady position
B. fluviatile	to 0.5 m	Ray Water Fern	Hardy	Needs shaded moist position
B. fraxineum	to 0.5 m		Hardy	Shaded, moist position; also requires warmth
B. gibbum	to 0.5 m	Palm Fern	Hardy	Develops short trunk, needs shade and moisture
B. minus	2 m	Soft Water Fern	Very if wet	Tuft-forming, needs wet soil, tolerates cold and direct sun
B. moorei	0.3 m		Medium	Well drained, composted, shady position
B. nudum	1.2 m	Fishbone Fern	Medium	Needs shade, moisture and acid soil
B. occidentale	to 1 m	Hammock Fern	Hardy	Needs sunny, wet site. Responds to feeding
B. orientale	1.2 m		Very	Needs warm moist conditions
B. patersonii	0.5 m	Strap Water Fern	Medium	Needs shade and water
B. spicant	0.1-0.7 m	Hard Fern	Very	Needs shade and acid soil; very cold hardy
B. watsii	1.2 m	Soft Water Fern	Very	Semi-protected site

Bolbitis
Lomariopsidaceae or Polypodiaceae

At a glance
Number of species: 44 (2 in Australia).
Natural habitat: Mainly tropical, mainly terrestrial, some on logs or rocks.
Hardiness: Generally hardy.
Habit: Mat forming.
Growth rate: Varies between species, generally slow.

Fronds: Great variation between species in frond shapes and sizes.

Comments: Some varieties are sterile and only reproduce vegetatively.

Culture

• Grows well in containers.
• Needs moist conditions.
• Usually prefers sheltered, shady positions.
• Terrestrial species prefer a high organic soil.
• The Australian species need a heated greenhouse in cooler areas.

Bommeria
Polypodiaceae

At a glance

Number of species: 4.
Natural habitat: Evergreen rock ferns.
Hardiness: Medium range.
Habit: Compact clump.
Comments: Fronds are hairy.

Culture

• Susceptible to overwatering.
• Needs good drainage.
• Needs air movement around foliage (keep plants well spaced).

Botrychium (Grape Fern/Moonwort)
Ophioglossaceae

At a glance

Number of species: Approximately 40 (2 Australian).
Natural habitat: Mainly temperate, terrestrial ferns.
Hardiness: Difficult.
Habit: Short fleshy rhizomes, not creeping.
Fronds: Fleshy foliage, not particularly attractive.
Comments: Sporangia occur on an erect pannicle resembling a bunch of grapes; a primitive group of ferns.

Culture

• Often difficult.

Byrsopteris

Included in *Arachnoides*.

Callipteris
Athyriaceae or Polypodiaceae

At a glance

Number of species: 3 (1 in Australia).
Natural habitat: Tropics (Africa to Australia).
Hardiness: Hardy in sheltered, moist positions.
Habit: Large terrestrial ferns.
Growth rate: Fast under humid, warm conditions.

Culture

• Prefers hot, humid conditions.
• Best plant in ground due to its vigour, but will grow in containers.
• Needs shelter in colder areas.

Camptosorus

Usually included in the genus *Asplenium*.

Campyloneurum — Plate 41

These are epiphytes, sometimes included in the genus *Polypodium*. Both temperate and tropical, with entire strap-like leaves.

Cardiomanes

Usually included in *Trichomanes*.

Cephalomanes
Hymenophyllaceae

At a glance

Number of species: Approximately 10 (1 in Australia).
Natural habitat: Wide distribution, mainly epiphytes on rocks or fern or tree trunks.
Hardiness: Generally delicate.
Habit: Epiphytes or lithophytes.
Growth rate: Slow to medium.
Comments: Sometimes included in *Trichomanes*.

Culture

• Best in a terrarium.
• Requires high humidity.

Ceratopteris (Water Fern, Floating Fern)
Parkeriaceae

At a glance
Number of species: 4.
Natural habitat: Warm climate, aquatic and muddy sites.
Hardiness: Hardy.
Habit: Floating, often with roots extending to mud below.

Culture
• Plant in ponds either free floating, or slightly submerged in pots.
• Propagate from buds forming on leaves.

Varieties
Common species include *C. cornuta*, *C. pteridoides*, *C. delatoidea* and *C. thalictroides*.

Cheilanthes — Plate 42
Adiantaceae

At a glance
Number of species: Many (approximately 12 in Australia).
Natural habitat: Warm climate, rock situations, in drier places.
Hardiness: Hardy, drought resistant.
Habit: Small creeping rhizomes.
Growth rate: Medium to fast.
Fronds: Small finely divided fronds, with reflexed margins and a covering of scales or hairs.
Comments: The structure of the fronds increases the plant's ability to cope with drier situations.

Culture
• Many need good light conditions, some need protection.
• Good drainage.
• Moist soil while growing.
• Some withstand, or even prefer, dryness during dormant period.
• Many prefer lower humidity than the average fern.

Varieties

Species	Height	Fronds
C. austrotenuifolia	to 0.5 m	3 pinnate, hairless
C. distans	to 0.3 m	Bipinnatifid, hairy
C. hirsuta	to 0.1 m	Bipinnatifid thin fronds
C. lasiophylla	to 0.2 m	Very hairy
C. sieberi	to 0.4 m	2–3 pinnate, hairless

Christella
Thelypteridacea or Polypodiacea

At a glance
Number of species: Approximately 60 (5 in Australia).
Natural habitat: Warm climate, mainly from South-East Asia.
Hardiness: *C. subpubescens* is hardy; others are rarely cultivated.
Habit: Mainly terrestrial.
Fronds: Lance-shape in outline, pinnatifid, mostly with pointed hairs on both sides of the frond.
Comments: Previously included in *Cyclosorus*, sometimes included in the genus *Thelypteris*.

Culture
Likes sunny open positions.

Varieties
C. dentata: Occurs in all states of Australia except Tasmania.
C. subpubescens: Hardy in warmer climates, but is sensitive to cold.

Cibotium (Tree Fern)
Dicksoniaceae

At a glance
Number of species: 15.
Natural habitat: Warm climates, America, Polynesia and Asia.
Hardiness: Very hardy.
Habit: Prostrate and larger, some tree ferns.
Growth rate: Varies but is generally good.
Fronds: To 0.6 m long.
Comments: Several species are highly prized by collectors.

Culture
• Sheltered moist position.
• Greenhouses in temperate climates.
• Easy to grow.
• Responds to feeding.
• Keep moist, mulch well with organic material.
• Good drainage is needed.
• Ideal as a tub plant.
• Propagate by spores.

Varieties

Species	Fronds	Hairs	Height	Culture
C. barometz	Glaucous underneath	Brown hairs on trunk	Low, 2 m trunk grows horizontally	Mulch, sun or shade
C. glaucum	Glaucous underneath, large	Yellow hairs on base of stipe	to 5 m tall	Warmth, very moist sheltered position
C. regale	Glaucous underneath	Cream hairs on trunk and stipe base	to 9 m tall	Acid soil, shade, good drainage, moisture
C. schiedei	Long and broad, weeping	Yellow-brown hairs on upper trunk	to 4 m tall	Adaptable, prefers shade and moisture

Cnemidaria

A prickly-stemmed tree fern to 1.2 m tall.
C. horrida grows in both tropical and temperate climates in shady moist places.

Colysis
Polypodiaceae

At a glance
Number of species: 30 (2 Australian).
Natural habitat: Warm climate rainforests.
Hardiness: Hardy.
Habit: Mainly terrestrial, with creeping rhizomes.
Fronds: Simple, pinnate or pinnatifid.
Comments: Is sometimes included in the genus *Polypodium*.

Culture
• Needs a moist shaded position.
• Propagated by spore or division.

Coniogramme
Hemionitidaceae or Polypodiaceae

At a glance
Number of species: 20.
Natural habitat: Tropical Africa, Asia and Polynesia.
Hardiness: Cultivated species are hardy (to southern Victoria).
Habit: Large ferns with creeping rhizomes.
Growth rate: Can be slow.
Fronds: 1–2 pinnate leaves, tall fronds.

Culture
• Cool moist conditions.
• Well drained, high organic soil.

Varieties

Plant	Height	Fronds	Comments
C. japonica (Bamboo Ferns)	to 0.7 m	Glossy dark green	Variegated type available
C. intermedia	to 1.2 m	Coarse dark green	Hardy in temperate climates

Crepidomanes
Hymenophyllaceae

A small filmy fern, sometimes included in *Trichomanes*. There are 12 species. Culture is as for *Trichomanes*.

Crypsinus
Polypodiaceae

At a glance
Number of species: Approximately 40 (1 in Australia).
Natural habitat: Mainly South-East Asia.
Hardiness: Hardy.
Habit: Epiphytes or rock ferns.
Growth rate: Average.
Fronds: Leathery, simple, pinnate or pinnatifid. Fertile fronds are dimorphic.

Culture
• Needs an open, well drained, organic soil or potting mix.
• A greenhouse is needed in cooler climates.

Varieties
C. simplicissimus is the most commonly grown species.

Cryptogramma (Rock Brake)
Cryptogrammataceae or Polypodiaceae

At a glance
Number of species: 4.
Natural habitat: Alpine and northern.
Habit: Small.
Fronds: Coarse texture.
Comments: Dimorphic.

Culture
• Likes acid soils, fairly bright light and good drainage.

Varieties

C. crispa (Parsley Fern): Grows well in acid soils.

Ctenitis
Polypodiaceae

At a glance
Number of species: 150 (1 Australian).
Natural habitat: Tropical, widespread, mainly Central and South America.
Hardiness: Hardy.
Habit: Medium to large, terrestrial, creeping rhizomes.
Growth rate:
Fronds: Leathery, 1–4 pinnate.
Comments: Was included in *Dryopteris*, but leaves are broader than *Dryopteris*.

Culture
• Moist temperate conditions.

Varieties
C. solanei (Florida Tree Fern): Likes humus rich soil, very sensitive to drying out.

Ctenopteris (Gipsy Fern)
Grammitidaceae

At a glance
Number of species: 200 (7 Australian).
Natural habitat: Tropical rainforests.
Hardiness: Delicate.
Habit: Short creeping rhizomes.
Comments: Resents disturbance.

Culture
• Requires very humid conditions such as aquaria.

Varieties
C. heterophylla (Gypsy Fern): Slow growing, rarely survives transplanting.

Culcita
Dennstaedtiaceae

At a glance
Number of species: 9.
Natural habitat: Mainly tropical rainforests (1 from Tasmania).
Hardiness: Medium, sensitive to cold and frosts.

Habit: Long creeping rhizomes.
Fronds: Broadly triangular, with soft hairy surface.
Comments: Easy to raise from spores.

Culture
• Likes well drained acid organic soils.

Varieties
C. dubia (Rainbow Fern): Vigorous, spreading, needs minimal attention.

Cyathea (Tree Fern) — Plates 43-47
Cyatheaceae

At a glance
Number of species: Approximately 110.
Natural habitat: Warm climate.
Hardiness: Many are hardy.
Habit: Evergreen.
Fronds: Very large, 2–3 pinnate leaves.
Comments: Many authorities group six genera *(Alsophila, Cnemidaria, Cyathea, Nephelea, Sphaeropteris* and *Trichipteris)* under this one genus, but many other authorities do not accept this division.

Culture
• Propagate from spores.

Varieties

Plant	Height	Comments
C. albifrons	to 3 m	Likes light, needs protection.
C. arborea	to 10 m	Requires moist, humid conditions and partial sun
C. baileyana	to 3 m	Slow growing, likes shade and moisture
C. brownii	to 5 m	Prefers partial sun, fast growing
C. cooperi	to 5 m	Prefers sun, fast growing
C. dealbata	to 3 m	Prefers abundance of water
C. howeana	to 2 m	Prefers cool semi-shady position
C. macarthuri	to 5 m	Requires sheltered position in temperate regions
C. marscescens	to 10 m	Hardy, likes moist position
C. robertsiana	to 7 m	Frost tender, protect from boring insects
C. woollsiana	to 5 m	Hardy, excellent tub plant

Cyclosorus

At a glance
Number of species: Recent reclassification groups many species into only two species. Some species have been placed in new genera. Other authors may classify some other species under *Christella*.

C. interruptus occurs in all Australian states except the south-east.

Cyrtomium (Holly Fern) — Plates 48, 49
Aspidiaceae or Polypodiaceae

At a glance
Number of species: 10 (Goudey gives 25).
Natural habitat: Warm climates, mainly eastern Australia.
Hardiness: Medium.
Habit: Scaly rhizomes.
Fronds: Leathery, holly-like shape.
Comments: Some authorities split this into two genera.

Culture
• Easily grown in greenhouses.
• Many tolerate coastal positions.

Varieties

Species	Size	Foliage	General
C. caryotideum	to 0.3 m	Pale green, prickly margins	Weeping
C. falcatum	to 0.5 m	Dark green, shiny	Fronds crested

Cystopteris (Bladder Fern)
Athyriaceae or Polypodiaceae

At a glance
Number of species: Approximately 18.
Natural habitat: Mainly temperate, rock ferns, usually in mountains.
Hardiness: Delicate.
Habit: Creeping rhizomes.
Fronds: Delicate and brittle, small to medium size.

Culture
• Needs shade.
• Moist cool position, or greenhouse.
• Prefers rocky embankments.

Varieties
C. filix-fragilis (Bottle Fern): Can be invasive in a glasshouse situation.
C. tasmanica (Brittle Bladder Fern): Requires damp rocky conditions.

Davallia (Haresfoot or Rabbitsfoot ferns) — Plate 50
Davalliaceae or Polypodiaceae

At a glance
Number of species: Approximately 40 (3 Australian).
Natural habitat: Mainly tropical and subtropical, Europe, Asia and Pacific. One is native to Victoria.
Hardiness: Hardy.
Habit: Long scale-covered rhizomes; mainly epiphytic, some rock ferns.

Culture
• Prefers temperatures between 18–22°C.
• Only a few species are frost hardy.
• Needs heavy watering while growing, but greatly reduced watering over winter.
• Aphis and scale are sometimes a problem.
• Ideal for hanging baskets.
• Propagate by spores, division or rhizome cuttings.

Varieties

Plant	Height	Fronds	General
D. bullata	to 0.2 m	3-4 pinnate	Deciduous, keep dry over winter
D. canariensis	to 0.6 m	3 pinnate	Hardy but frost tender, slower growing but longer lived
D. corniculata	to 0.6 m	3-4 pinnate	Rarely grown
D. denticulata	to 1 m	3 pinnate	Needs greenhouse in cool climates, deciduous over winter
D. divaricata	to 1 m	3 pinnate	New fronds are dark mauve, needs greenhouse in cool climates
D. embolostegia	to 1.2 m	4 pinnate	Light green, young growth reddish, needs greenhouse in cool climates
D. feejeensis	to 1 m	3-5 pinnate	Several forms are grown, varying in size, colour and form. Very popular in basket culture. Dwarf forms are also grown. Generally needs a greenhouse in cool climates
D. griffithiana	to 0.5 m	3-4 pinnate	Easily grown, often confused with D. mariessii
D. mariessii	to 0.3 m	3-4 pinnate	The most popular and commonly grown variety; hardy and cold resistant
D. plumosa	to 0.5 m	2-3 pinnate	Large leathery fronds, needs warmth, humidity and ventilation
D. pyxidata	to 0.8 m	2-3 pinnate	Easy to grow, native to Australia
D. solida	to 1 m	3-4 pinnate	Needs greenhouse in cool climates
D. tasmanii	to 0.5 m	3-4 pinnate	Very hardy and cold resistant, does poorly in cool climates

Davallodes
Polypodiaceae

At a glance
Number of species: 11.
Natural habitat: South-East Asia and New Guinea.
Hardiness: Mountains.
Habit: Epiphytes.

Culture
• Propagated from spores.

Dennstaedtia (Cup Fern)
Dennstaedtiaceae or Polypodiaceae

At a glance
Number of species: Approximately 70 (1 Australian).
Natural habitat: Tropical and subtropical, normally wet forests.
Hardiness: Hardy, easy to cultivate.
Habit: Creeping rhizomes, large or medium sized clumps, terrestrial.
Leaves: Delicate.
Comments: Hairy rhizomes; a primitive group of ferns.

Culture
• Requires moist humid conditions.

Varieties
D. davalliodes (Lacy Ground Fern): Best contained in tub, very hardy.

Dicksonia (Tree Fern) —Plate 51
Dicksoniaceae

At a glance
Number of species: Approximately 30 (2 Australian).
Natural habitat: Mountains, mainly warm climates —some cooler parts.
Hardiness: Hardy to very hardy.
Habit: Tree fern.
Growth rate: Medium to fast.
Fronds: 2-4 pinnate, lance-shaped, bases of fronds have stiff hairs.
Comments: Considered more primitive than *Cyathea*. Stipes on *Dicksonia* are smooth, on *Cyathea* stipes are rough.

Culture
• Protect from wind.
• Needs moist soil.
• Needs shade in warmer climates.
• Prefers shade in cooler climates.

Varieties

Species	Hardiness	Growth	Trunk	Height	Conditions
D. antarctica (Soft Tree Fern)	Hardy	Fast	Thick	to 12 m	Moist and sheltered
D. fibrosa (Golden Tree Fern)	Hardy	Slow	Thick	to 6 m	Cool and moist
D. herbertii	Medium	Fast	Slim	to 3 m	Needs some shade
D. lanata	Hardy	Easy	Semi upright		Moist and cool
D. sellowiana			Slim	to 5 m	
D. squarrosa (Rough Tree Fern)	Hardy	Easy	Slim	to 3 m	Part sun, moist
D. youngiae (Bristly Tree Fern)	Hardy	Easy	Slim	to 5 m	Warm, moist and sheltered

Dicranopteris
Gleichiaceae

At a glance
Number of species: 10 (1 Australian).
Natural habitat: Warm climate.
Hardiness: Hardy.
Habit: Long creeping rhizomes.
Fronds: Divided, hard or wiry in texture.

Culture
• Sun loving.
• Needs warm, moist soil.
• Difficult to grow in containers.

Varieties
D. linearis is the only Australian species.

Dictymia (Strap Fern)
Polypodiaceae

At a glance
Number of species: 4 (1 Australian).
Natural habitat: Pacific, warm climate.
Hardiness: Hardy.
Habit: Creeping rhizomes.
Growth rate: Slow but steady.
Fronds: Stiff, erect, simple, strap-like, leathery, dark green.

Culture
• Needs shade and humidity.
• Do not crowd—requires air movement around the foliage.

Varieties

D. brownii: Easily grown in an open, chunky, high organic potting mix.

Didymochlaena (Tree Maidenhair)

At a glance
Number of species: 1 *(D. trunculata).* ·
Natural habitat: Worldwide, wet tropical areas, in gullies.
Hardiness: Tender when small, hardy once established.
Habit: Crown-forming.
Fronds: Large and bipinnate, lustrous green.

Culture
• Keep warm when young.
• Sheltered position or greenhouse in temperate areas.

Diplazium
Athyriaceae or Polypodiaceae

At a glance
Number of species: Over 300 (8 Australian).
Natural habitat: Mainly warm climates, wet mountain forests, some are temperate climate plants.
Hardiness: Tender to hardy (drying out is the biggest problem).
Habit: Large, terrestrial, short creeping rhizomes, some like mini tree ferns.

Culture
• High humidity in the air is essential for good results.
• Best as greenhouse plants in cool climates.
• Need shade.
• Need protection from slugs and snails when young.
• Soil must remain moist.

Varieties
D. australe (Austral Lady Fern): Very susceptible to drying out.
D. esculentum (Edible Fern): Extremely hardy, even becoming a weed once established in moist soil.

Diplopterygium (Giant Scrambling Fern)
Gleicheniaceae

At a glance
Number of species: 20 (1 from Queensland).
Natural habitat: A terrestrial fern on the edge of forests or embankments.
Hardiness: Hardy in warm sunny positions.
Habit: Long creeping rhizomes, thin and wiry, like a giant *Gleichenia.*
Growth rate: Can be fast in the ground.
Fronds: Pinnatifid.

Culture
• Sunny position.
• Moist soil.

Varieties
D. longissimum: The only Australian species, grows between 1 and 3 m tall in the ground. It also adapts to growing in tubs.

Doodia (Rasp Ferns)
Polypodiaceae or Blechnaceae

At a glance
Number of species: 15 (6 Australian).
Natural habitat: Tropical and temperate; Ceylon, Australia and Polynesia; wet forests, among rocks.
Hardiness: All very hardy.
Habit: Dwarf ferns, scaly rhizomes, normally short rhizomes.
Growth rate: Average to fast.
Fronds: Normally a rough texture, pinnate, sometimes dimorphic. Young fronds are often pinkish.

Culture
• No strong sunlight.
• Medium to cool environment (but not too cold).
• Needs moist conditions.
• Propagate by division or spores.
• Ideal among rocks.

Varieties
Commonly grown varieties include:
  D. aspera (Prickly Rasp Fern): New growth attractive pink.
  D. caudata (Small Rasp Fern): Hardy, attractive young pink fronds.
  D. maxima (Giant Rasp Fern): New growth attractive rosy colour.
  D. media (Common Rasp Fern): New growth

attractive red colour.

D. squarrosa: Easily grown in protected moist situations.

Doryopteris
Polypodiaceae

At a glance
Number of species: Approximately 25.
Natural habitat: Tropics, open forests, rocky places.
Hardiness: Hardy to very hardy.
Habit: Small, short creeping rhizomes.
Growth rate: Average.
Fronds: Palmate or simple.
Comments: Stipes are black and thin.

Culture
• Same as for *Pteris.*
• pH can be important—the pH requirement varies between species.

Varieties
D. concolor: Glossy hand-shaped fronds, needs moist warm conditions.
D. pedata (Hand Fern): The most commonly grown variety.

Drynaria
Polypodiaceae

At a glance
Number of species: Approximately 20 (3 Australian).
Natural habitat: Moist tropical and subtropical.
Hardiness: Hardy.
Habit: Epiphytes (some rock ferns), thick scaly rhizomes.
Growth rate: Some can be fast growers in warm situations.
Fronds: There are two types, one short and shaped like an oak leaf, the other pinnate or pinnatifid.
Comments: Sometimes called *Polypodium.*

Culture
• Many tolerate mild frosts.
• Several varieties are drought tolerant once established.
• Most need good light.
• Generally they need a greenhouse or other protection in a cool climate.

Dryopteris (Wood Fern/Shield Fern) — Plates 52–55
Polypodiaceae or Aspidiaceae

At a glance
Number of species: Approximately 150 (1 Australian).
Natural habitat: Temperate and tropical.
Hardiness: Many hardy to very hardy.
Habit: Terrestrial, short rhizomes—thick and scaly.
Fronds: Leathery, 1-6 pinnate, some are deciduous.

Culture
• Needs moist well drained soils.
• Most need acidic soil high in organic material.

Gleichenia (Coral Fern) — Plate 56
Gleicheniaceae

At a glance
Number of species: 10 (6 Australian).
Natural habitat: Mainly tropical, wet exposed sites, Asia and Pacific. Two from Tasmania.
Hardiness: Hardy once established in moist soils.
Habit: Thicket-forming with creeping rhizomes.
Growth rate: Can be slow in cultivation.
Fronds: Leathery leaves, pinnules are small.

Culture
• Hard to transplant.
• Must be wet soil.
• Requires a well lit position.
• Best in ground (difficult to grow in pots).

Goniophlebium
Polypodiaceae

At a glance
Number of species: 2 Australian.
Natural habitat: Warm climates.
Hardiness: Hardy.
Habit: Large epiphytes with creeping rhizomes.
Growth rate: Average to fast.
Comments: Sometimes included in *Polypodium* or *Schelolepis.*

Culture
• Needs ventilation around foliage.
• Requires good drainage.
• Feed only with slow release fertilisers.
• In cool regions they need a greenhouse.

- Ideal in baskets.
- Slaters and earwigs are sometimes a problem.

Varieties
G. verrucosum: A long-lived fern with a weeping habit. It is excellent in a basket, requiring warmth, humidity and a well drained organic potting mix.

Gonocormus
Hymenophyllaceae

At a glance
Number of species: 10 (2 Australian).
Natural habitat: Mainly warm wet forests.
Hardiness: Poor in cultivation.
Habit: Small with long creeping rhizomes.
Comments: Often included in *Trichomanes.*

Culture
As for *Trichomanes.*

Grammitis (Finger Fern)
Grammitidaceae

At a glance
Number of species: 150 (10 Australian).
Natural habitat: Alpine areas.
Hardiness: Poor to average.
Habit: Erect or creeping rhizomes, sometimes with hairs but no scales.
Growth rate: Slow.

Culture
- Most are difficult to grow.
- The best chance of success is in a terrarium.

Gymnocarpium (Oak Fern)
Polypodiaceae

At a glance
Number of species: 2 or 3.
Natural habitat: Northern temperate areas.
Hardiness: Delicate.
Habit: Slender creeping rhizomes.
Fronds: Tripinnate.
Comments: Can be deciduous.

Culture
- Requires a well drained moist soil.
- Shade is essential.

Varieties
G. dryopteris: Roots should never be allowed to dry out.
G. robertianum: Requires a high pH soil.

Gymnogramme

Generally included in *Coniogramme.*

Gymnopteris

Sometimes included in either the genus *Cheilanthes* or *Notholaena.*

Helminthostachys
Ophioglassaceae

At a glance
Number of species: 1.
Natural habitat: South-East Asia.
Habit: Creeping rhizome.

Culture
- Do not fertilise.
- Never allow roots to dry out.

Hemionitis — Plate 57
Hemionitidaceae or Polypodiaceae

At a glance
Number of species: 8.
Natural habitat: Tropical (mainly American); thick forests and rocky sites.
Hardiness: Sensitive to hardy.
Habit: Small terrestrial, sometimes rock dwellers.
Fronds: Palmate to entire.

Culture
- Some varieties need light.
- Require moist position.
- Need warm humid conditions.
- Propagate by division, buds or spores.

Varieties
H. arifolia (Heart Fern): Has heart-shaped fronds, is difficult to grow in large pots, needs a soil pH of 7 or higher.
H. elegans: Has palmate fronds and requires a soil pH of 7 or less.
H. palmata: Has palmate fronds similar in shape to strawberry leaves.

Histiopteris
Dennstaedtiaceae or Polypodiaceae

At a glance
Number of species: Approximately 50 (6 in Australia).
Natural habitat: Terrestrial, tropical and temperate, in rainforest clearings.
Hardiness: Very hardy.
Habit: Creeping rhizomes with scales; forms clumps.
Growth rate: Strong.
Fronds: Up to 1 m tall.
Comments: Rhizomes are hairy; can become a weed.

Culture
• Needs wet soil.
• Withstands full sunlight.
• Culture is easy if soil is wet.
• Caterpillars are sometimes a problem.

Varieties
It is often difficult to distinguished between species.
H. incisa: Grows up to 1.5 m tall in shady places.

Humata
Polypodiaceae

At a glance
Number of species: Approximately 50 (2 Australian).
Natural habitat: Tropical.
Hardiness: Hardy in warm climates.
Habit: Epiphytic, small, creeping rhizomes—similar to *Davallia.*
Comments: Leathery.

Culture
• Needs wet soils.
• Greenhouse culture in temperate climates.
• Grows best in hanging baskets.

Varieties
H. griffithiana: Easier to grow in containers than many others.
H. tyermanii: Has distinctive silver-coloured rhizomes, one of the hardier and more frequently cultivated varieties.

Hymenophyllum (Filmy Fern)
Hymenophyllaceae

At a glance
Number of species: Approximately 300 (14 in Australia).
Natural habitat: Wet places.
Hardiness: Relatively hardy root system. In dry conditions the top may die but when watered the roots will regrow.
Habit: Slender rhizomes—often a small root system; epiphytes and rock plants.
Growth rate: Medium to fast.
Fronds: Small, delicate (only 1 cell thick).
Comments: Primitive group.

Culture
• Best in wet places.
• Best in warm climates, but will grow in temperate areas.
• Excellent terrarium plant.
• Not strongly competitive.

Hypolepis
Dennstaedtiaceae or Polypodiaceae

At a glance
Number of species: Approximately 50 (6 Australian).
Natural habitat: Tropical and subtropical; wet open sites, along watercourses and in forest clearings
Hardiness: Generally hardy.
Habit: Creeping rhizomes, terrestrial.

Culture
• Most need shade.
• Caterpillars are sometimes a problem.
• Sometimes grown in greenhouses.

Lastreopsis (Shield Fern) — Plate 58
Aspidiaceae or Dryopteridaceae

At a glance
Number of species: Approximately 35 (13 Australian).
Natural habitat: Warm climate mainly, though some in Tasmania.
Hardiness: Average, though some are very hardy.
Habit: Mainly terrestrial; short rhizomes.
Leaves: 2-3 pinnate.

Culture
• Moist but well drained—not saturated (some are

sensitive to extremes of moisture).
• Most like high organic soils.
• Shade is generally preferred, though some tolerate full sun.

Lecanopteris (Ant Fern)

From South-East Asia, long-lived epiphytic plants requiring well drained soil.

Lemmaphyllum
Polypodiaceae

At a glance
Natural habitat: Tropical and temperate Asia and the Pacific.
Hardiness: Hardy.
Habit: Epiphytes with long creeping rhizomes.
Growth rate: Fast.
Fronds: Small, entire (undivided), dimorphic.
Comments: Long-lived.

Lepisorus
Polypodiaceae

At a glance
Natural habitat: Subtropics to temperate regions.
Hardiness: Hardy.
Habit: Small epiphytic ferns with creeping rhizomes.
Fronds: Entire (undivided).

Leptolepia

At a glance
Number of species: 1.
Natural habitat: Rainforest to dry woodland.
Hardiness: Hardy to very hardy.
Habit: Wiry rhizomes.
Growth rate: Slow.
Leaves: Delicate, 3–4 pinnate.

Culture
• Requires a sheltered garden position.
• Grows well in baskets.

Varieties
L. novae-zealandiae: To 0.5 m tall with fine-cut lacy foliage.

Leptopteris (Crepe Fern)
Osmundaceae

At a glance
Number of species: Approximately 7.
Natural habitat: Tropical and temperate rainforests, Western Pacific.
Hardiness: Delicate.
Habit: Eventually grow trunks like tree ferns.
Fronds: To 1 m long, very thin, sometimes transparent when moist.
Comments: Highly sensitive to chemicals (even fluoridated water). A primitive group, sometimes included in the genus *Todea*.

Culture
• Must have a shaded wet position.
• As for *Todea*.

Leucostegia
Polypodiaceae

At a glance
Number of species: 2.
Natural habitat: South-East Asia and Polynesia.
Hardiness: Hardy once established.
Habit: Normally terrestrial, sometimes epiphytes, thick fleshy rhizomes.
Fronds: 3–4 pinnate.

Culture
• Good drainage is essential.
• Warmth is needed (greenhouse conditions required in cool climates).

Varieties
L. pallida: Grows easily in a basket in a warm and humid environment.

Lindsaea (Screw Ferns) — Plate 59
Lindsaeaceae

At a glance
Number of species: 200 (14 Australian).
Natural habitat: Varies; tropical and temperate, rainforests to drier areas.
Hardiness: Generally hardy.
Habit: Creeping rhizomes.
Fronds: 1–3 pinnate, pinnae often similar in appearance to maidenhair pinnae.

Comments: Stipes have a few scales at the base.

Culture
• Varies according to variety.

Varieties
L. odorata: Has a not-so-pleasant musky odour.

Llavea
Cryptogrammataceae or Polypodiaceae

At a glance
Number of species: 1.
Natural habitat: Central America, moist soil, often on limestone and in rocky places.
Hardiness: Semi-hardy.
Habit: Terrestrial.
Leaves: Stiff, pale green, long and narrow.

Culture
• Requires a greenhouse in Victoria.
• Can be grown outdoors in subtropics.
• Needs high pH soils.
• Needs wet conditions.

Varieties
L. cordifolia: Yellow/green pinnate leaves, to 0.7 m tall, should be kept dry over dormant period in winter.

Loxogramme
Polypodiaceae

Not cultivated.

Loxsoma
1 species from New Zealand.
Grows in open moist forests; long creeping rhizomes, pale green fronds, difficult to cultivate.

Loxsomopsis
Small group of ferns from Central America similar to *Loxsoma.*

Lunathyrium (Lady Fern)
Athyriaceae or Polypodiaceae

At a glance
Number of species: 40 (1 Australian).
Natural habitat: Temperate rainforests and wet sclerophyll forests.
Hardiness: Hardy.
Habit: Clump-forming, terrestrial.
Leaves: 1–2 pinnate.
Comments: Can be deciduous in cold weather.

Culture
• Requires shade.
• Needs a well drained but wet organic soil.
• pH requirement can vary between species.

Lygodium
Climbing ferns; approximately 30 species (4 Australian); mainly on the edges of forests, a few grow in swamps, most are hardy and easily grown.

Macroglena (Filmy Fern)
Hymenophyllaceae

At a glance
Number of species: 12 (2 Australian).
Natural habitat: Tropical and temperate.
Hardiness: Medium hardy.
Habit: Short or long creeping rhizomes, thick rhizomes.
Leaves: Delicate (1 cell thick).
Comments: Often included in *Trichomanes.*

Culture
• Needs constant humidity.
• Best in pots or terrariums.
• Low light conditions are generally preferred.

Macrothelypteris
Thelypteridaceae

At a glance
Number of species: 6 (2 Australian).
Natural habitat: Warm climate.
Hardiness: Hardy, but frost tender.
Habit: Terrestrial.
Fronds: Normally 3–4 pinnate.
Comments: Often included in *Thelypteris.*

Culture
• Prefers well lit situation (some even tolerate direct sun).
• Prefers moist soils.
• Wind can sometimes be a problem.

Marattia (Potato Fern)
Marrattiaceae

At a glance
Number of species: Approximately 60 (1 Australian).
Natural habitat: Tropics and temperate, southern hemisphere.
Hardiness: Many are hardy.
Habit: Large, many up to 4 m or more tall.
Fronds: Thick and fleshy, to 3 m long, normally 3–4 pinnate.

Culture
• Grown occasionally in greenhouses.
• Well lit situations.
• Needs sheltered moist position, warmth and humidity.
• Many varieties are easy to grow.
• Propagated by spores or division.

Marsilea (Water Clover or Nardoo) — Plate 62
Marsileaceae

At a glance
Number of species: Approximately 65 (7 Australian).
Natural habitat: Aquatic and swamp land, tropics and subtropics.
Hardiness: Hardy.
Habit: Float in deep water; root into mud in shallow water.
Fronds: Leaves like a four-leaved clover.

Culture
• Grows in mud, or a pot of soil immersed in water.
• Propagate by division or pieces of rhizome.

Varieties
M. drummondii (Nardoo): An Australian native fern, commonly grown in water gardens.

Matteuccia (Ostrich Fern)
Polypodiaceae

At a glance
Number of species: 3.
Natural habitat: Temperate.
Hardiness: Very hardy.
Habit: Large ferns.

Growth rate: Generally vigorous.
Fronds: Pinnate, resembling fishbone ferns.

Culture
• Full sun or part shade.
• Rich/fertile soils preferred.
• Moist or not too dry soils.
• Most prefer acid, loamy soils.
• Transplants easily.

Mecodium

From the filmy fern family (Dennstaedtiaceae), frequently included in *Hymenophyllum*.

Meringium

In the Dennstaedtiaceae family, also often included in *Hymenophyllum*.

Merinthosorus

Epiphytic; large ferns from warm climates.

Microgonium
Hymenophyllaceae

At a glance
Number of species: 12 (4 Australian).
Habit: Rhizomes are hairy and medium creeping.
Leaves: Simple or lobed.
Comments: Has no roots.

Microgramma

Generally included in *Polypodium*.

Microlepia
Polypodiaceae

At a glance
Number of species: Approximately 45.
Natural habitat: Tropics or subtropics, worldwide.
Hardiness: Some hardy, some not.
Habit: Terrestrial, large, medium to long rhizomes.
Leaves: Soft, hairy, upright fronds, light green.

Culture
• Normally grown in a greenhouse.
• Most prefer shady places.
• Hardier varieties will thrive outside in mild climates if shaded.

Microsorum
Polypodiaceae

At a glance
Number of species: Approximately 60 (6 Australian).
Natural habitat: Mainly warm climates, mainly from Asia.
Hardiness: Generally hardy to very hardy.
Habit: Creeping rhizomes on trees or rocks; scales on rhizomes; mainly epiphytes.
Fronds: Simple and strap-like.

Culture
• Cold sensitive.
• Needs warmth.
• Needs ventilation and humidity.
• Many varieties are excellent in baskets or pots.
• Many are easily grown.

Nephelea (Tree Fern)
Cyatheaceae

At a glance
Number of species: 30.
Natural habitat: America; warm or temperate climates.
Hardiness: Hardy.
Habit: Tree fern.
Fronds: Spiny dark green leaves, leaf stalks have sharp black spines.
Comments: Sometimes included in *Cyathea*.

Culture
• Needs warmth and moisture to grow well.
• Best in well lit position, perhaps with filtered sunlight.

Varieties
N. mexicana (also known as *Cyathea mexicana*): Grows to 6 m tall, has a thick trunk, with long black spines, large lacy fronds to 3 m, growing best in warmer climates.

Nephrolepis (Sword Fern/Fishbone) — Plates 60, 61
Oleandraceae or Polypodiaceae

At a glance
Number of species: Approximately 30 (6 Australian).

Natural habitat: Tropics and subtropics, dry open forests or on the edge of rainforests.
Hardiness: Many very hardy.
Habit: Tuft forming, creeping rhizomes/stolons, terrestrial, some epiphytic.
Growth rate: Fast.

Culture
• Needs lots of water in warmer months (too much water in a greenhouse can cause rotting though).
• Very drought tolerant.
• Most are sensitive to severe frost or cold.
• Survives better in potbound state than many other ferns.
• Excellent indoors.
• The finer leaved varieties are the more difficult to grow.
• Propagate by division, spores or tissue culture.

Varieties

Plant	Height	Comments
N. cordifolia	to 1 m	Very hardy, adapts most situations
N. hirsutula	to 1.8 m	Large fronds, frost tender
N. falcata		Attractive forked pinnae, frost tender

Niphidium
Polypodiaceae

At a glance
Number of species: Approximately 10.
Natural habitat: Mainly on trees and rocks, in a variety of habitats.
Hardiness: Average.
Habit: Medium size epiphytes.
Fronds: Entire (simple shaped).

Culture
• Needs good light but not excessive sun.
• Requires plenty of air movement around the plant.
• Water well in summer, keep drier in cooler months.
• Suited to pots or baskets.

Varieties
N. crassifolium: 0.5–1.5 m, needs glasshouse protection.

Notholaena (Cloak Fern)
Polypodiaceae

At a glance
Number of species: Approximately 60.
Natural habitat: Warm climate, rock-loving.
Hardiness: Generally hardy.
Habit: Small, clump-forming.
Leaves: Leaves chaffy or hairy.
Comments: Sometimes included in *Cheilanthes*.

Culture
- Needs good ventilation.
- Requires a well drained soil.
- Needs good light levels.

Varieties

Species	Height	Fronds	Needs
N. sinuata	to 0.7 m	1 pinnate	Perfect drainage, good light, good air movement
N. standleyi	to 0.3 m	2–3 pinnate	Well ventilated and good light, soil pH of 7 or above

Oeontrichia

At a glance
Number of species: 4 (2 from Queensland).
Natural habitat: Warm climate from New Guinea to New Caledonia, wet sites.
Hardiness: Hardy in the right conditions.
Habit: Rhizomes.
Fronds: Divided.

Culture
- Needs a well drained, high organic soil.
- Requires a moist environment.
- Shade is essential.

Oleandra
Oleandraceae

At a glance
Number of species: Approximately 40.
Natural habitat: Worldwide in high organic soils and rotting wood.
Hardiness: Average.
Habit: Stiff rhizomes growing in the air, supported by stilt-like roots.
Fronds: Simple, tapered at both ends like an oleander leaf.

Culture
- Requires warmth and humidity.

- Good levels of light are important.

Onoclea
Polypodiaceae

At a glance
Number of species: 1.
Natural habitat: Terrestrial, in wet exposed places, USA and Asia.
Hardiness: Very hardy, can become a weed.
Habit: Creeping rhizomes.
Growth rate: Can be fast.
Fronds: 1–2 pinnate.
Comments: Can be deciduous in cool climates.

Varieties
O. sensibilis: Large fronds shaped like an oak leaf.

Onychium (Claw Fern)
Cryptogrammataceae or Polypodiaceae

At a glance
Number of species: 4.
Natural habitat: Subtropical Africa and Asia, damp exposed sites.
Hardiness: Most are semi hardy.
Habit: Small, terrestrial, creeping rhizomes.
Growth rate: Can be fast.

Culture
- Needs moist soils and high humidity.
- Prefers bright light.
- Normally grown in a greenhouse.
- Can be difficult to keep in good condition (often becoming weedy in appearance).

Varieties
O. japonicum (Carrot Fern): Easily grown in cultivation.

Ophioglossum
Ophioglossaceae

At a glance
Number of species: Approximately 30.
Natural habitat: Tropical and temperate, usually in damp muddy places.
Hardiness: Epiphytic types are easier to grow.
Habit: Short rhizomes, small plants, mainly terrestrial, some epiphytic.

Leaves: Mostly undivided leaves.
Comments: Have a symbiotic relationship with a fungus.

Culture
• Needs wet position or a humid greenhouse.
• Most are difficult to establish.
• Terrestrial varieties are difficult to grow.

Varieties
O. pendulum: Can be difficult to establish, but once established in an epiphytic potting mix grows well.
O. petiolatum: Easier to grow, but must remain moist at all times during the growing season, and dry when dormant.

Osmunda (Flowering Fern) — Plate 63
Osmundaceae or Polypodiaceae

At a glance
Number of species: 10.
Natural habitat: Temperate and tropical, wet sites, mainly in the open, on the edge of water, in swamps or open woodlands.
Hardiness: Very hardy.
Habit: Clump forming.
Growth rate: Average to fast.
Fronds: Coarse but attractive, mainly deciduous.
Comments: Primitive family which also contains *Todea* and *Leptopteris.*

Culture
• Deep rooted.
• Needs moist, high organic soil.
• Requires shade.
• Spore should be sown fresh (it does not generally store well).

Varieties

Species	Height	Fronds	Colour
O. banksiifolia	to 0.8 m	1 pinnate	Light green
O. cinnamomea	to 1.5 m	1–2 pinnate	Blue-green, changing to brown
O. regalis	to 2.5 m	2 pinnate	Green

Paesia

At a glance
Number of species: Approximately 12.
Natural habitat: Mainly tropical rainforests, particularly in clearings.

Hardiness: Generally hardy.
Habit: Small, terrestrial, with long slim rhizomes.
Growth rate: Can be fast.
Leaves: Fine, 4 pinnate.

Culture
• Cold hardy.
• Will withstand a semi-exposed position.
• Requires a well lit site.
• Propagated by division.

Varieties
P. scaberula: The most commonly grown, a very hardy fern with sweet smelling fronds; it can however become a weed if not controlled.

Paraceterach
Adiantaceae or Hemionitidaceae

At a glance
Number of species: 2 (both Australian).
Natural habitat: Rocky inland dry sites.
Hardiness: Very hardy, drought tolerant.
Habit: Small, clump forming, with scale-covered creeping rhizomes.
Growth rate: Can be fast.
Leaves: Many scales on the lower surface, will grow outdoors in temperate climates.

Culture
• Good ventilation is required.
• Outdoors in the tropics, in greenhouses in temperate climates.

Parathelypteris
Often included in *Thelypteris.*

Pellaea (Cliff Brake)—Plate 64
Adiantaceae or Polypodiaceae

At a glance
Number of species: Approximately 80 (2 Australian); 35 according to Goudey.
Natural habitat: Mainly temperate and subtropics, open forests, rocky sites.
Hardiness: Hardy to very hardy.
Habit: Small terrestrial.
Growth rate: Average to fast.
Leaves: Leaves often leathery with scattered scales on the lower surface.
Comments: Some varieties can be deciduous in cold weather.

Culture
- Grows well in rock gardens.
- Prefers filtered sun or an open position.
- Once established will take drier conditions than many other ferns.
- Some grown in greenhouses.

Varieties

Species	Common name	Height	Requirements	Colour
P. atropurpurea	Purple Rock Brake	to 0.5 m	Alkaline soils	Blue-green
P. falcata	Sickle Fern	to 0.6 m	Shade to filtered sun	Green
P. rotundifolia	Button Fern	to 0.2 m	Acid soil	Dark green
P. viridis	Green Cliff Brake	to 0.3 m	Well drained alkaline soil	Bright green

Phanerophlebia
Polypodiaceae

Some authorities recognise this as *Cyrtomium*.

Phegopteris

Often included in *Thelypteris*.

Phlebodium
Polypodiaceae

At a glance
Number of species: Approximately 6.
Natural habitat: Varies.
Hardiness: Some can be difficult, others are very hardy.
Habit: Mainly epiphytes with thick creeping rhizomes.
Growth rate: Varies according to variety.
Fronds: Generally blue-green colour.
Comments: Has been undergoing reclassification in recent years. Is sometimes included in *Polypodium*.

Culture
- Prefers warm, moist conditions.
- Some grow much easier than others.
- Potting mixes should be coarse and well draining.

Varieties
P. aureum (Golden Polypody): Grows between 0.3 and 1.5 m tall, has pinnatifid fronds, and is relatively easy to grow. Several different forms are available.
P. decumanum: Grows 0.3 to 1.2 m tall, has pinnatifid fronds, more difficult than *P. aureum*.

Phyllitis—Plate 65
Polypodiaceae

At a glance
Number of species: 9.
Natural habitat: Temperate to tropical.
Hardiness: Generally hardy.
Habit: Mainly small.
Comments: Simple strap-like leaves; sometimes included in *Asplenium*.

Culture
- As for *Asplenium*.

Phymatosorus—Plate 66
Polypodiaceae

At a glance
Number of species: Approximately 15 species (3 Australian).
Natural habitat: From East Africa, Australia and the Pacific.
Hardiness: Generally hardy.
Habit: Mainly epiphytes, clump-forming, with creeping rhizomes.
Fronds: Entire to pinnatifid.
Comments: Previously included in *Microsorum* and *Phymatodea*.

Culture
- Potting mixes should be coarse.

Varieties
P. diversifolius (Kangaroo Fern): Pinnatifid fronds up to 0.5 m long.
P. scandens (Fragrant Fern): Pinnatifid fronds up to 0.4 m long.

Pilularia (Pillwort)
Marsiliaceae

At a glance
Number of species: 61 (1 Australian).
Natural habitat: Swamps in temperate climates, in mud rather than water.
Hardiness: Hardy.
Habit: Long thin creeping rhizomes, upright fronds.
Fronds: Fronds are slender or grass like.

Culture

• Most grow in mud, though some will grow submerged or free floating.

Pityrogramma (Gold Fern/Silver Fern)
Hemionitidaceae or Polypodiaceae

At a glance
Number of species: 16.
Natural habitat: Mainly tropical.
Hardiness: Hardy to very hardy.
Habit: Terrestrial.
Fronds: Undersurface covered with silver, white or gold coloured powder; mainly bipinnate.
Growth rate: Average to fast.

Culture
• Generally needs full or filtered sunlight.
• Requires good drainage.
• Normally grown in greenhouses.
• Simple needs.
• Can be grown in the open in warm climates.

Varieties
P. calomelanos and *P. chrysophylla:* Both to 0.4 m tall are two of the easiest to grow.
P. triangularis: Needs shade.

Platycerium (Staghorn/Elkhorn)—Plates 67, 68
Polypodiaceae

At a glance
Number of species: Approximately 15 (3 Australian).
Natural habitat: Warm climate.
Hardiness: Some hardy (Australian species are hardy as far south as Melbourne).
Habit: Epiphytic, spreading and drooping.
Growth rate: Medium to fast.

Culture
• All need protection from frost (some won't tolerate temperatures below 15°C).
• In cool climates keep dry over winter.
• Generally there are few pests, though sometimes moths, mealy bugs, beetles or lacewings can be a problem.
• Propagate easily by division.
• Spore germinates but is difficult to keep growing.

Varieties
P. bifurcatum (Elkhorn Fern): Has a brown or green sheath of infertile fronds covering the roots. The fertile grey-green fronds are strap-like with a Y-shaped tip, up to 1 m in length.
P. grande (Staghorn Fern): Has a green sheath of infertile fronds covering the roots and broader lobed fertile fronds.

These are the two most commonly grown in Australia. They are also two of the most cold hardy species, being able to survive temperatures to 0°C or even lower.

Pleopeltis

This is sometimes included in the genus *Polypodium.*

Pleuromanes
Hymenophyllaceae

At a glance
Number of species: 3 (1 tropical Australia).
Habit: Long creeping rhizomes.
Fronds: Broad, bipinnatifid.

Culture
Requires terrarium, slow growing.

Pleurosorus (Blanket Fern)
Aspleniaceae or Polypodiaceae

At a glance
Number of species: 2 Australian (all states).
Natural habitat: Semi-exposed rock crevices, in drier places.
Hardiness: Drought tolerant.
Habit: Coarse erect rhizome, small fern.
Fronds: Usually pinnate.

Culture
• Similar to the hardier Asplenium species.
• Avoid high humidity.
• Suited to a small pot or a sheltered rockery position.
• Do not overwater.

Pneumatopteris
Thelypteridaceae or Polypodiaceae

At a glance
Number of species: Approximately 75 (3 Australian); Melbourne University gives 75.
Natural habitat: Mainly Malaysia, in forests near streams. One species native to Tasmania.
Hardiness: Hardy.
Habit: Clump-forming with erect or short creeping rhizomes.
Fronds: Bipinnatifid.
Comments: Rarely cultivated.

Polyphlebium (Filmy Fern)
Hymenophyllaceae

At a glance
Natural habitat: Wet forests and gullies of south-east Australia and New Zealand.
Habit: Epiphytes.
Comments: Often included in *Trichomanes*.

Culture
• As for *Trichomanes*.

Polypodium (Polypody)—Plates 69, 70
Polypodiaceae

At a glance
Number of species: Very large group; recently divided into 20 or more different genera.
Natural habitat: Varied, mainly tropical, some temperate. Anything from moist acid to dry limestone soils.
Hardiness: Many are hardy.
Habit: Mainly epiphytic, with creeping rhizomes, both large and small.
Growth rate: Many are slow.

Culture
• Needs coarse soil.
• Do not overwater.
• Ventilation or good air movement is important.
• Many are good as indoor plants.

Varieties
P. australe (Southern Polypody): One of the most commonly grown.

Polystichum (Shield Fern)—Plates 71–73
Aspidiaceae or Polypodiaceae

At a glance
Number of species: Approximately 175 (5 in Australia).
Natural habitat: Tropics to the subantarctic.
Hardiness: Hardy to very hardy.
Habit: Varies.
Growth rate: Medium to fast.
Fronds: Varies from tripinnate to strap-like.

Culture
• Best in moist soils with partial shade, though some tolerate full sun.
• Outdoors and greenhouse grown.
• Propagated by spores. Some propagated by plantlets.

Varieties

Plant	Height	Comments
P. australiense	to 1.2 m	Easy to propagate, likes shady areas
P. proliferum	to 1 m	Likes tubs, is very hardy, tolerates sun

Pronephrium
Thelypteridaceae

At a glance
Number of species: Approximately 70 (2 Australian).
Natural habitat: Rainforests in India, South-East Asia and the Pacific, generally beside water.
Hardiness: Generally hardy as far south as Victoria.
Habit: Short to medium creeping rhizomes.
Fronds: Pinnate.

Culture
• Grows in mild temperate climates outdoors.
• Will grow in containers or the ground.

Pseudodrynaria
Polypodiaceae

At a glance
Number of species: 1.
Natural habitat: Tropical Asia.
Hardiness: Hardy.
Habit: Epiphytes up to 2 m diameter with thick woolly rhizomes.
Fronds: Pinnatifid, leathery and dark green.
Comments: Previously included in *Aglaomorpha*—similar to *Drynaria*.

Culture

• Tolerates the cold if kept dry.
• Needs good light conditions.

Pteridium (Bracken)
Dennstaedtiaceae or Polypodiaceae

At a glance
Number of species: 1–12 varieties.
Natural habitat: Varied, worldwide.
Hardiness: Very hardy.
Habit: Clump-forming, spreading rhizomes.
Growth rate: Fast.
Comments: Mature foliage is poisonous; usually a weed.

Culture
• Transplants readily.
• More commonly considered a weed than a garden plant, though some varieties are more attractive than others (some tropical varieties cultivated at times).

Pteris (Brake/Dish Fern/Table Fern)
Pteridaceae or Polypodiaceae

At a glance
Number of species: Approximately 280.
Natural habitat: Mainly tropical, varied, dry to wet, full shade to sunny, varied situations.
Hardiness: Generally hardy and adaptable to different situations.
Habit: Terrestrial, clump-forming.
Growth rate: Can be fast.

Culture
• Needs lots of water while growing.
• Do not allow to become potbound.
• Roots will die if they dry out.
• No direct or hot sun.
• Temperate climate species tolerate cold, others are cold sensitive.
• Can get aphis on stipes.
• Normally spore propagated, though some can be divided.

Varieties

Plant	Leaves	Height	General
P. comans	3 pinnate	to 2 m	Likes cool moist fernery
P. tremula	3 pinnate	to 2 m	Hardy fern indoors or out
P. umbrosa	1 pinnate	to 2 m	Likes moist shade and high amounts of mulch
P. vittata	1 pinnate	to 1 m	Hardy, likes sun, well drained position

Pyrrosia (Felt Fern)—Plate 75
Polypodiaceae

At a glance
Number of species: Approximately 100 (5 in Australia).
Natural habitat: Asia and South-East Asia, a few in Africa and the Pacific; medium to high rainfall forests, often in clearings.
Hardiness: Hardy, drought resistant.
Habit: Epiphytic, creeping rhizomes and rock inhabiting, most are small.
Growth rate: Fast.
Leaves: Thick fleshy simple fronds covered with hairs on lower surface.
Comments: Leathery leaves, normally simple.

Culture
• Needs good light.
• Tropical species need heated greenhouses in temperate regions.

Reediella
Hymenophyllaceae

At a glance
Number of species: 5 (2 in Australia).
Natural habitat: Warm climates.
Hardiness: Small epiphytes, long creeping rhizomes.
Leaves: Pinnatifid to bipinnatifid, upright.

Regnellidium

Aquatic ferns related to *Marsilea*.

Rumohra (Leather Fern)
Polypodiaceae or Davalliaceae

At a glance
Number of species: 1 (some say up to 6).
Natural habitat: Tropics and temperate in Southern hemisphere.
Hardiness: Some varieties cold hardy to Tasmania; generally hardy once established.
Habit: Creeping rhizomes, usually terrestrial (sometimes epiphytic), tend to grow smaller in cold climates.
Fronds: Tripinnate, leathery.
Growth rate: Can be slow to establish.

Culture

• Grow as an epiphyte on a slab or in a basket.
• Does not like root disturbance.

Sadleria—Plate 76
Polypodiaceae

At a glance
Number of species: 6.
Natural habitat: Hawaii.
Hardiness: Hardy in warm climates.
Habit: Low tree ferns.
Growth rate: Medium.

Culture
• Needs a greenhouse or good protection in temperate climates.

Salvinia
Salviniaceae

At a glance
Number of species: Approximately 10.
Natural habitat: Warm climate.
Hardiness: Can be a weed.
Habit: Aquatic, free floating and rootless.
Growth rate: Extremely fast in tropical areas, may choke waterways.
Comments: Small leaves.

Schizaea
Schizaeaceae

At a glance
Number of species: 30 (7 Australian).
Natural habitat: Mainly warm climate on poor acid soils; sometimes alpine or rocky, several cooler climate species.
Hardiness: Hardy once established.
Habit: Small tufts or short creeping hairy rhizomes.
Fronds: Erect and narrow, widening to a comb-like section on top.
Comments: A fungal symbiosis exists. At first glance it does not appear like a fern.

Culture
• Do not tolerate root disturbance.
• Some take full sun.
• Best grown as transplants from wet sites where they are growing on top of rock—this way root disturbance is minimal. Spore propagation is difficult due to fungal symbiosis.

Scyphularia

At a glance
Number of species: 8.
Natural habitat: South-East Asia and the Pacific.
Habit: Epiphytes and rock ferns with long slender rhizomes.

Varieties
S. pycnocarpa: An excellent basket fern and tolerates a fair amount of sun.

Selenodesmium
Hymenophyllaceae

At a glance
Number of species: 10 (2 Australian).
Natural habitat: Widely distributed.
Habit: Rhizomes with erect fronds.
Comments: Frequently included under *Trichomanes.*

Culture
As for *Trichomanes.*

Varieties
S. obscurum: Does not tolerate disturbance.

Selliguea
Polypodiaceae

At a glance
Number of species: 8: 2 are cultivated in Australia.
Natural habitat: Subtropical to temperate.
Hardiness: Hardy in tropical areas but need protection in cooler climates.
Habit: Epiphytes with creeping rhizomes.

Culture
• Needs humidity and good drainage.
• Needs well ventilated position.

Varieties
S. feei: Has entire leaves, grows to 15 cm.

Sphaerocionium
Hymenophyllaceae

At a glance
Number of species: Approximately 50 (1 Australian).
Natural habitat: Mainly South American.
Habit: Rhizomes long, creeping.

Varieties
S. lyallii: A small filmy fern, grows in dense mats.

Sphaeropteris (Tree Fern)
Cyatheaceae

At a glance
Number of species: Approximately 120.
Natural habitat: Tropical.
Hardiness: Fairly hardy once established.
Habit: Sometimes very large.
Comments: Members of this group sometimes classified under *Cyathea*, fronds up to 6 m long.

Varieties
S. cooperi: When full grown is hardy in temperate regions; also known as *Cyathea cooperi.*
S. medullaris: Frond bases and scales black, very hardy.

Sphaerostephanos
Formerly part of *Cyclosorus.*

Stenochlaena (Swamp Fern)
Blechnaceae or Polypodiaceae

At a glance
Number of species: 5.
Natural habitat: Africa to Pacific, swamps in warm climates.
Hardiness: Hardy in warm climates.
Habit: Climbing epiphytes with long rhizomes.
Growth rate: Can be fast.
Fronds: Large, pinnate; sterile fronds are lance-shaped, fertile fronds are linear.
Comments: Can tend to become a weed in ideal conditions.

Culture
• Usually warm humid conditions.
• Cold sensitive.

• Moist soils.
• Likes to climb.

Sticherus (Fan Fern)—Plate 77
Gleicheniaceae

At a glance
Number of species: 3 in Australia (2 in eastern Australia).
Natural habitat: Mainly in warm rainforests to dry forests, along watercourses or dry embarkments.
Hardiness: Medium once established.
Habit: Long creeping slim rhizomes, gets higher with age.
Growth rate: Slow.
Fronds: Fronds fan-shaped, pinnules oblong to linear.

Culture
• Never fertilise!
• Do not transplant well, do not like any root disturbance.
• Best in wet, semi-exposed positions.

Varieties

Plant	Fronds	Height	General
S. flabellatus	1-4 tiers of umbrella-like pinnae	to 2 m	Semi-sun
S. lobatus	Fan shaped fronds	to 2 m	Takes some sun
S. tener	1-4 tiers of umbrella-like pinnae	to 2 m	Dislikes disturbance

Tectaria
Polypodiaceae or Aspidiaceae

At a glance
Number of species: Approximately 200 (4 from Queensland).
Natural habitat: Tropics, most in wet forests, some on limestone soils.
Hardiness: Hardy.
Habit: Large terrestrial or rock ferns, short creeping rhizomes.
Growth rate: Some are slow to establish.
Fronds: Simple, pinnatifid or divided.

Culture
• Easy to grow.
• Some are slightly frost tender, others extremely frost tender.
• Best grown under glass in temperate climates.

Thyrsopteris

Related to *Dicksonia* and *Cyathea*, in the family Thyrsopteridaceae.

Thelypteris
Thelypteridaceae or Polypodiaceae

At a glance
Number of species: Approximately 200 (1 Australian).
Natural habitat: Throughout the tropics, some from northern temperate climates, mainly swamps and rainforests.
Hardiness: Generally hardy.
Habit: Long or short creeping rhizomes.
Leaves: Pinnate to bipinnate, often leathery.
Comments: Formerly part of *Cyclosorus*.

Culture
• Withstands sun.
• Needs moist soil.
• Best grown in the ground.

Varieties

Plant	Leaves	General
T. confluens	2 pinnate	Likes moist sunny conditions
T. patens var. *lepida*		Likes moist sunny situation

Todea (Tree Fern)—Plate 78
Osmundaceae

At a glance
Number of species: 2 (1 Australian).
Natural habitat: Very wet sites, mainly rainforests, gullies and streams.
Hardiness: Very hardy.
Habit: Large trunks.
Growth rate: Medium, grows well in cultivation.
Fronds: Leathery leaves; primitive tree fern.

Culture
• Grows best in moist gardens or well watered tubs.
• Will take some full sun.

Varieties
T. barbara (King Fern): Excellent tub fern, very hardy, attractive.

Trichipteris

Tree ferns from warm and temperate climate America; in the Cyatheaceae family.

Trichomanes (Filmy Fern)
Hymenophyllaceae

At a glance
Number of species: Approximately 300.
Natural habitat: Very wet sites, distributed worldwide.
Hardiness: Poor in cultivation.
Habit: Long wiry rhizomes forming a clump.
Fronds: Can absorb water readily; this often results in a small root system. Fronds are delicate, they may often die off but the plant will normally survive and regrow when wet.
Comments: Sometimes called *Cardiomanes*.

Culture
• Difficult in cultivation.
• Must have high humidity.
• Perhaps best grown in a terrarium.

Varieties
T. johnstonense: Grows well in tubs, likes dark humid positions.
T. venosum: Likes humidity, grows well in fibrous soils.

Trogostolon
Davalliaceae or Polypodiaceae

At a glance
Number of species: 1.
Natural habitat: Philippines.
Hardiness: Not very hardy.
Habit: Slender long creeping rhizome.
Growth rate: Slow growing.
Comments: Related to *Davallia*.

Culture
• As for *Davallia*.

Vittaria (Grass or Ribbon Fern)
Vittariaceae or Polypodiaceae

At a glance
Number of species: Approximately 50 (2 Australian).

Natural habitat: Tropics and subtropics, on trees and rocks in rainforests.
Habit: Clustered slender rhizomes, leaves in tufts.
Growth rate: Slow growing.
Fronds: Linear.

Culture

• Best in an epiphytic soil medium.
• Best in a moderate heated greenhouse.

Woodsia

Polypodiaceae

At a glance

Number of species: Approximately 40.
Natural habitat: Temperate and cool temperate.
Hardiness: Medium.
Habit: Small ferns.
Comments: Rootstocks tufted.

Culture

• Likes rocky sites.
• Suited to rock or alpine gardens.

Woodwardia (Chain Fern)—Plate 79

Polypodiaceae

At a glance

Number of species: 12 (3 Australian).
Natural habitat: Temperate, some warm climate; wet places—forests, grasslands, streams, etc.
Hardiness: Hardy.
Habit: Terrestrial, long or short creeping rhizomes.
Growth rate: Fast.

Culture

• Moist soils are essential.
• Greenhouse grown.

Varieties

Plant	Leaves	Height	General
W. areolata	1 pinnate	to 1 m	Sun tolerant, acid soil, glossy
W. fimbriata	2 pinnate	to 2 m	Needs shade, dark green
W. orientalis	2 pinnate	to 2.5 m	Takes some sun
W. radicans	2 pinnate	to 2 m	Cold hardy
W. virginicia	2 pinnate	to 0.5 m	Bronze-coloured new growth

Appendices

1 Glossary

Caudex Woody upright trunk, usually referring to tree ferns.

Crozier The curled-up young fern frond, in the process of opening up.

Dimorphic Of fronds, occurring in two different shapes or forms.

Epiphyte Plants which grow in the air, attached to another plant but not parasitic to that plant (e.g. growing on a tree fern trunk).

Filiform Thread-like.

Glabrous Smooth, not having any hairs.

Glaucous Having a powdery covering, normally shades of white or blue.

Indusium A membrane which covers the place where spores are produced.

Lithophyte A plant which grows on rock.

Linear Long and narrow shape with parallel sides.

Palmate Similar shape to a palm leaf, divided into five leaf segments all starting from the same point.

Petiole The leaf stalk, that is, the stem which goes from the ground, or the trunk, to the start of the leaflets or pinnules.

Pinnate Where frond or leaf is divided, with leaflets being arranged on either side of the central rib. For example, 2-pinnate means divided twice.

Pinnule Each individual segment of a divided frond or leaf is called a pinnule.

Prothallus The flat, green, heart-shaped growths which develop from the germinating spore. Eggs and sperm are produced and fertilise on the prothallus, giving rise to new plants.

Pubescent Having a covering of soft hairs.

Rachis Midrib of the frond or leaf blade on a fern.

Rhizome A type of creeping stem which fronds grow from, frequently but not always underground. Long creeping rhizomes have large gaps between each point from which a frond emerges. Short creeping rhizomes have short gaps between fronds.

Scale A dry, flat, papery structure, leaf or plate like.

Stipe A term used to describe the petiole on ferns (i.e. the leaf blade).

Terrestrial Growing in the ground.

Undivided A leaf or frond with a simple or entire shape—not pinnate.

Pinnate leaf (*Adiantum* sp.)

Undivided or simple leaf (*Microsorium* sp.)

tufted rhizome

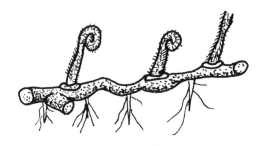

long creeping rhizome

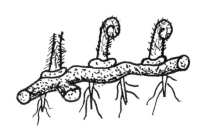

medium creeping rhizome

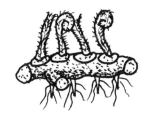

short creeping rhizome

Types of rhizome

2 Further reading

There are three things to note about the literature available on ferns:

1. The available literature is not comprehensive. As yet, there is no book written which covers all ferns, and much about ferns simply has not been written.

2. No book can be considered the 'ultimate authority' on ferns. Because of the high level of disagreement between the experts, even the most accurate works frequently contradict each other.

3. There has been a lot of inaccurate writing produced in the past. It is not uncommon for fern books and articles to be written by people more skilled in journalism, photography or drawing than in botany or horticulture. You are well advised to consider the background and qualifications of the author you are reading.

The following books can be recommended:

General
Encyclopedia of Ferns by David Jones (Lothian, Melbourne)
Ferns to Know and Grow by F.G. Foster (Hawthorn, New York)
Fern Growers' Manual by Hoshizaki (Knopf, New York)

Ferns: Wisley Handbook 32 (Royal Horticultural Society, London).
Ferns: A Handbook (Brooklyn Botanic Gardens, New York).
A Handbook of Ferns by Chris Goudey (Lothian, Melbourne)
Ferns to Know and Grow (Knopf, New York)

Specialised
Maidenhair Ferns in Cultivation by C. Goudey (Lothian, Melbourne)

Cultural Practice
Growing Media by Handreck and Black (NSW University Press, Sydney)
Plant Science by Hartmann (Prentice Hall, New Jersey)
Safer Pest Control by Rogers (Kangaroo Press, Sydney)
Growing Australian Natives in Pots by Blombery (Kangaroo Press, Sydney)
The Native Plant Expert by John Mason (Australian Horticultural Correspondence School)

Landscaping
Practical Gardening and Landscaping by Blombery (Angus & Robertson, Sydney)
Native Gardens by Molyneaux (Nelson, Melbourne)
The English Garden School by Alexander (Michael Joseph, London)

The above books are available from:
Horticulture and Leisure Services
Mail Order Book Service
264 Swansea Rd, Lilydale, 3140.

3 Fern nurseries

NSW
Afrale Pty Ltd, Beach Rd, Woodburn 2472
(066) 82 2588
Australian Native Ferns, PO Box 45, Helensburgh 2508
(042) 94 1375
Cascade Fernery, 88 Vineyard St, Warriewood 2102
(02) 997 4255
Fallons Nursery, Main Arm Rd, Mullumbimby 2482
(066) 84 5393
Great Eastern Plants, 57 Pacific Hwy, Coffs Harbour 2450

Geekie Fern Nursery, 6 Nelson St, Thornleigh 2120
(02) 484 2684
Green Frond Nursery, 39 Fisher Rd, Maraylya 2765
Illawarra Native Nursery, 'Dusodie' via Dungog 2460
(049) 95 9272
Kanget Native Nursery, RMB 9, Gloucester Rd, Wingham 2429
Marleys Ferns, Mt Kuringai 2080
(02) 457 9168

Tallawalla Fernery, RMB 2775, Nelson Bay Rd, Salt Ash via Newcastle 2301

Townsend Street Fernery, 274 Townsend St, Albury 2640

Wagga Fern Grove, 49 Copeland St, Wagga Wagga 2650 (Mail order)

Wattons Native Ferns, 32 Pacific Hwy, Bennetts Green 2290

Victoria

Alans Flat Plant Farm, Tomkins Lane, Allans Flat 3691

Austral Ferns, 25 Cozens Rd, Lara 3212

Australian Fern & Orchid Distributors, 27 Old Hereford Rd, Mt Evelyn 3796 (03) 736 3585

Beasley's Nursery, 195 Warrandyte Rd, Doncaster East 3109

Bloomers Fernery & Nursery, cnr Sth Gippsland Hwy & Amy's Track, Foster 3960

Cool Waters Fern Nursery, Beech Forest 3237 (052) 37 3283

Fernacres Nursery, PO Box 143, Whittlesea 3757 (057) 86 5481

Fern City, 412 Canterbury Rd, Ringwood 3134 (03) 874 8399

Fern Glen, Garfield Nth 3814 (056) 29 2375

Fernland, Lot 1, Milners Rd, Lang Lang 3984 (059) 97 8313

Fletcher's Fern Nursery, 62 Walker Rd, Seville 3139 (059) 64 4680

John Corrie, 7 Eileen St, Viewbank 3084 (03) 459 7367

Melaleuca Nursery, Pearsall Rd, Inverloch 3996

G & A Williams, cnr Aldershot Rd, Langwarrin 3910

Ridge Road Fernery, Weeaproinah 3237 (052) 35 9383

Tanjenong Nursery, Mt Dandenong Rd, Olinda 3788

Tree Action, Lot 3, Rougheads Rd, Leongatha Sth 3953 (056) 64 3259

Waridarrah Fernery, Lot 5, Russells Rd, Woodend Nth 3442 (054) 27 2937

Whelans Fernery, Swan Reach 3903 (051) 56 4220

Queensland

Baffle Creek Nursery, c/- Lowmead 4676

Barrier Reef Nursery, PO Box 14, Babinda 4861 (070) 67 5226

Bob Delaney, 4 Ahern St, Labrador 4215

De Witte's Tassell Fernery, PO Box 107, Kuranda 4872 (070) 93 7129

Dundarra Wholesale Nursery, Dunning St (PO Box 20), Palmwoods 4555. Ph (074) 45 9481

Fern Growers of Australia, 155 Fryars Rd, Eagleby 4207. Ph (07) 287 2965

Fernland Wholesale Nursery, 174 Dowding Rd, Oxley 4075. Ph (07) 375 5731

Heatons Wholesale Fern Nursery, Burnside Rd, Nambour 4560. Ph (074) 41 1574

Hilders Nursery, PO Box 18, Upper Stone, via Ingham 4850

McPherson Nursery, Back Creek Rd, Rathdowney 4287. Ph (075) 44 3157

Mountaindale Ferns, PO Box 91, Palmwoods 4555

Mt Nebo Plant Nursery, Mt Nebo Rd, Mt Nebo 4520. Ph (07) 289 8175

Sonters, 364 Boundary Rd, Thornlands 4164. Ph (07) 207 8311

Stagworld, cnr Boundary & Redland Bay Rds, Thornlands 4164. Ph (07) 207 7765

South Australia

Aussie Plant Growers, Womma Rd, Penfield 5121

Conboys Nursery, PO Box 1047, Mt Gambier 5290

Craigburn Nursery, 156 Coromandel Pde, Blackwood 5051 (08) 278 8019

Fairview Fern Supplies, Seaview Rd, Yatala Vale 5126 (08) 251 4650

Peter Engels, 1700 Main Rd Nth, Salisbury Plains 5109 (08) 258 2166

Lasscocks Pty Ltd, 334 Henley Beach Rd, Lockleys 5032 (08) 352 2004

Marks Fern Nursery, Cherry Gardens Rd, Cherry Gardens 5157 (05) 388 2113

Nottle's Wholesale Fern Nursery, 17 Coolabah Dve, Murray Bridge 5253

Tasmania

Bicheno Nursery, PO Box 43, Bicheno 7215 (003) 75 1449

Liffey Valley Fernery, Liffey Rd, Liffey 7301 (003) 97 3437

Western Australia

Canningvale Wholesale Nursery, 44 Birnam Rd, Canningvale 6155

Maces Fern Nursery, Lot 28 Coachwood Way, Gelorup 6230

Portaferry Farm, 2684 Albany Hwy, Kelmscott 6111 390 3960

Sonters, 69 Ross Rd, Wanneroo 6065

New Zealand

Crumps Fern Nursery, 64 Trigg Rd, Whenuapai, Auckland

Jacketts Nursery, Wildmans Rd, Metueka, Nelson

Moa Park Nursery, PO Box 401, Greymouth

Nikau Gardens, 411 Nayland Rd, Stoke, Nelson

Talisman Nurseries Ltd, Ringawhati Rd, RD Otaki

4 Suppliers of equipment and materials

Shade houses
A.D. Spring Mfg, 154 Bellevue Pde, Carlton NSW 2218
W.A. Young & Co, 120 Rozelle Ave, Edwardstown, SA 5039
Solar Hot Houses, c/- PO, Epsom Vic. 3551
Superspan, PO Box 169, Mordialloc Vic. 3195
Mesh FMP, Factory 11, 212 Grovenor Rd, Braeside Vic. 3195
Shed Scene, Settlement Rd, Thomastown Vic. 3074

Greenhouses
Sage Horticultural, 121 Herald St, Cheltenham Vic. 3192

Growing Systems of Australia, 645 Burwood Hwy, Vermont Sth Vic. 3133
Solar Hot Houses, c/- PO, Epsom Vic. 3551
Greenspan, 13 Porter St, Ryde NSW 2112
Shed Scene, Settlement Rd, Thomastown Vic. 3074
Qyntek, 13 Brougham St, Eltham Vic. 3095

Propagation equipment
Sage Horticultural, 121 Herald St, Cheltenham Vic. 3192
Solar Hot Houses, c/- PO Epsom Vic. 3551

5 Fern clubs and societies

Australia
Fern Society of Victoria
PO Box 45, Heidelberg West 3081
Fern Society of Western Australia
c/- Mrs Bromley, 73 Point Walter Rd, Bicton 6157
Fern Society of South Australia
PO Box 711, GPO, Adelaide 5001
Tasmanian Fern Society
c/- Julie Haas, 72 Bush Creek Rd, Lenah Valley 7008
Society for Growing Australian Plants
Fern Study Group
The Secretary, M. Woollett, 3 Currawang Place, Como West NSW 2226

New Zealand
Nelson Fern Society of New Zealand
9 Bay View Rd, Otawhai, Nelson

United Kingdom
British Pteridological Society
c/- Mr A. Busby, 42 Lewisham Rd, Smethwick, Warley, West Midlands B66 2BS

USA
American Fern Society
c/- Mr M. Cousens, Faculty of Biology, University of West Florida, Pensacola, Florida 32504
Los Angeles International Fern Society
c/- 14895 Gardenhill Dve, La Mirada, California 90638

6 Where to see ferns

In the wild

Victoria
Near Melbourne: Dandenongs, Macedon, Kinglake, Healesville, Warburton
Rainforests in East Gippsland, Wilsons Promontory

South Gippsland
Otways
Subalpine Rainforests, e.g. Cumberland Falls and Cement Creek

New South Wales
The Blue Mountains
Morton National Park, 50 km south of Wollongong
New England National Park, 75 km east of Armidale
Dorrigo National Park, 127 km east of Armidale

Australian Capital Territory
Tidbinbilla Nature Reserve, 40 km south-west of Canberra
Queensland
Cuninghams Gap National Park, 110 km south-west of Brisbane
Lamington National Park, 120 km south-east of Brisbane
Tamborine Mountain National Park, 70 km south-east of Brisbane
Carnarvon Gorge National Park, 466 km north-west of Brisbane (rare ferns)
Eungella National Park, 48 km east of Mackay
Palmerston National Park—between Innisfail and Ravenshoe
Cape Tribulation
Mossman River Gorge
Tully Falls

Western Australia
Norseman Gorge in the Kimberleys (also other gorges in the Kimberleys)
South-Western Rainforests

South Australia
Warrawong Sanctuary, Mylor, Adelaide Hills

Tasmania
Approximately 40% of Tasmania is covered by rainforests which have ferns growing in them.
Mount Field National Park
Hastings Caves
Cradle Valley
Elephant Pass

In gardens

Victoria
Ripponlea, 192 Hotham St, Elsternwick, Melbourne.
A National Trust Property, open to the public daily (except Monday and Tuesday over winter). The extensive Victorian gardens contain a massive, recently restored fernery, perhaps the best example to be seen in Australia.
Ballarat Botanic Gardens
Geelong Botanic Gardens
Wangaratta Garden Club Fernery, Merriwa Park
Royal Botanic Gardens, Melbourne
The Rhododendron Gardens, The Georgian Rd, Olinda

New South Wales
Royal Botanic Gardens, Sydney—Pyramid House
Burrendong Arboretum

Australian Capital Territory
Canberra Botanic Gardens Fern Gully

Queensland
Botanic Gardens—Rockhampton
Kuranda Railway Station, Cairns (the station is famous for its ferns).

Western Australia
Kings Park Fern House, Perth

South Australia
Royal Botanic Gardens, Adelaide—Palm House—new conservatory
Royal Botanic Gardens, Mt Lofty. This is the best public collection in SA.

Tasmania
Botanic Gardens, Hobart—Fern House

7 Recommended ferns

Sun tolerant varieties

Ferns are rarely suited to full sun, though the following will perform reasonably well with some direct sunlight in morning and afternoon. They will need filtered sunlight in the hottest part of the day and at the hottest time of the year.

Hardy in full sun if soil remains moist and humidity is high:
   Blechnum occidentale
   Cibotium glaucum
   Dicksonia antarctica
   Dryopteris noveboracensis

Osmunda (all varieties)
Pteridium aquilinum
Sphaeropteris cooperi

Hardy with some shading in the hottest part of the day:

Davallia trichomanoides
Doodia media
Dryopteris erythrosora
Nephrolepis cordifolia
Pellaea (most species)
Platycerium (most species)
Polypodium aureum
Polystichum polyblepharum
Pteris cretica
Pteris vittata
Todea barbara

Dry soil ferns

These ferns will tolerate drier and more exposed conditions, but will still need some water:

Blechnum occidentale
Davallia trichomanoides
Nephrolepis cordifolia
Polypodium aurea
Pteridium aquilinium
Pteris cretica
Pteris vittata
Woodwardia fibriata

Colour in foliage:

Adiantum: new fronds are red, but turn green as they grow

Blechnum: new fronds red but generally turn green later

Adiantum raddianum variegatum: white variegated

Alsophila tricolor (syn. *Cyathea dealbata*): white under fronds

Polypodium aristatum variegatum: white and yellow variegation

Athyrium niponicum pictum: greyish and purple variegation

Ferns for terrariums

Annogramma leptophylla
Asplenium flabellifolium
Asplenium trichomanes
Blechnum penna-marina

Cardiomanes reniform
Doodia caudata
Hymenophyllum sp.
Leptopteris sp.
Macroglena caudata
Pleurosorus rutifolius
Pyrossia rupestris
Selaginella (most species)
Trichomanes (most species)

Ferns for hanging baskets

Adiantum aethiopicum
Asplenium bulbiferum
Asplenium flabellifolium
Blechnum fluviatile
Blechnum gibbum
Cyrtomium falcatum
Davallia (most sp.)
Doodia aspera
Doodia caudata
Doodia media
Drynaria rigidula and cultivars
Humata sp.
Lygodium japonicum
Microsorium diversifolium
Microsorium scandens
Microsorium punctatum
Microgramma (several sp.)
Nephrolepis cordata and cultivars
Nephrolepis exalata and cultivars
Phlebodium aureum and cultivars
Phymatosurus (several sp.)
Polypodium (many species including *australe* and its cultivars, and *formosum*)
Pyrossia (many species)
Pteris cretica cultivars
Rumohra adiantiformis
Sadleria cyatheoides
Scyphularia pentaphylla

Ferns for wet conditions

Angiopteris evecta
Athyrium filix-femina
Blechnum fluviatile
Blechnum minus
Blechnum nudum
Blechnum wattsii
Cyathea australis
Dennstaedtia davalloides

Dicksonia antarctica
Dicksonia herbertii
Histiopteris incisa
Ligodium microphyllum
Nephrolepis biserrata

Osmunda regalis
Pteris umbrosa
Thelypteris confluens
Todea barbara

8 Further information—Correspondence courses

The Australian Horticultural Correspondence School conducts a variety of courses for the fern enthusiast.

Growing Ferns

This course teaches the identification and culture of ferns in all situations from growing in the ground to baskets and tubs. Watering, feeding, potting soils, propagation and lots more are all covered. All types of fern are dealt with including epiphytes, ground ferns, rock dwellers, tree ferns and even ferns for indoor plants.

Australian native ferns

Learn what ferns occur naturally in Australia, how to identify them, where to get more information, how to grow and propagate them, and lots more.

Bush garden design

After developing an understanding of the workings of natural environments, you learn how to create innovative plans for low maintenance bush gardens. Eight lessons teach you about native plants including ferns, how to mix them together in a balanced way to create desired effects, how to build rockeries, ponds, patios, etc. and lots more.

Most courses take about 2 hours per week for 12 months to complete.

Further information including fees can be obtained from:
AHCS, 264 Swansea Rd, Lilydale Vic. 3140, ph (03) 736 1882; or PO Box 2092, Nerang East, Qld 4211, ph (075) 304 855.

Index

Nov. 21, 2007